Woodworking in the Home/Volume Four

Collins Step-by-Step Guides

Woodworking in the Home

Volume Four

by Adrienne and Peter Oldale

Collins / Glasgow and London

Printed in Great Britain by
C. Tinling & Co. Ltd.,
London and Prescot

SBN 00 435461 3

Filmset by Keyspools Ltd.,
Golborne, Lancs.

Contents

Contents (continued)

Tool Kit

One good tool is worth half-a-dozen poor ones. Nearly anything can be made with a saw, a hammer, a screwdriver and a chisel.

The best rule when buying tools is to get only those which you need at once. Do not buy large sets or kits at first. But those which you do buy should be of the very best quality. Cheap tools are a waste of money and you cannot do good work with them.

It is impossible for the ordinary householder to check tools for quality. The only guides are the price and the brand name. The field of toolmaking is so competitive that you usually get exactly what you pay for. A saw costing 10s. will be of far worse quality than one costing £2 *even though they may look exactly alike*. Good steel looks just the same as poor steel. A cheap wooden handle can be covered in good-looking paint or plastic.

A good chisel will take a razor-edge. Make sure then that you have a safe place to keep it. Always put your tools away with a cover over the cutting edges. Rust is a real enemy to sharpness. You may not be able to see it, but a film of rust blunts an edge considerably. A simple wipe with an oily rag after use will prevent this.

Sharpening is an important task with chisels and planes, but quite easy to tackle, as you will see on p. 92.

For the time being though, you do not need such tools. Here is a short list of those you should start with. As you need more, we will describe them separately.

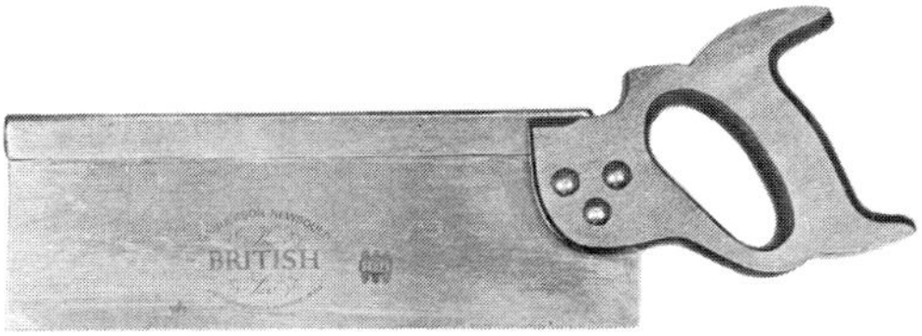

Saw–Tenon The tenon saw is a general purpose tool. In fact you can make almost anything in wood with it. It has a stiffened back parallel to the teeth. It is roughly a foot long and has 10 to 14 teeth to the inch.

Saw–Panel Though you do not need one of these as well as a tenon saw, many people already have one. It is better for cutting strips and planks but is not as versatile as the tenon saw. Roughly 2 ft. long and tapering, it is most useful with about 10 teeth per inch.

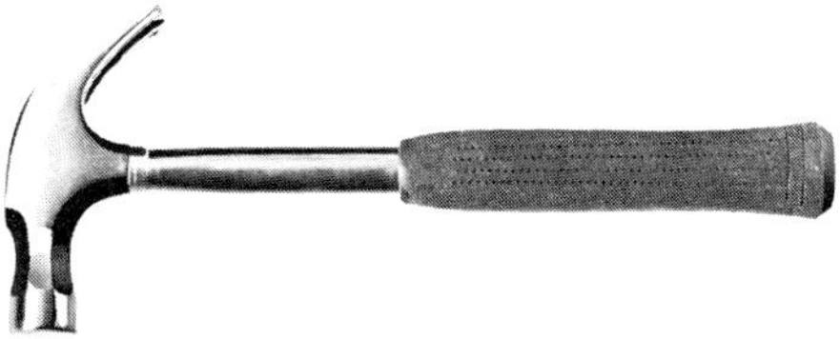

Hammer Again, most householders will already have one. But the rule about buying good quality still applies, as you must have a really strong handle with a securely fixed head. Loose heads are dangerous but almost unknown with good makes. It is useful to choose one with curved claws to extract wrongly-driven nails.

Screwdriver Another common household tool. The tip is not ground sharp, but flat, so that it will not slip out of the screw slot.

Strictly speaking you should use a screwdriver which exactly matches the screw you are driving; a counsel of perfection that few of us attain! One with a $\frac{1}{4}$ in. wide tip fits most screws. A smaller one comes in handy at times. If you buy one, choose one of the 'electrician's' type as it can be used for other purposes too.

Spirit Level One of the commonest jobs is putting up shelves. As these look terrible if they are not level you should have a spirit level right from the start. But there is no need to buy a large, expensive one at first. A cheap one may be quite serviceable, because the bubble glasses are much the same in dear or cheap sorts.

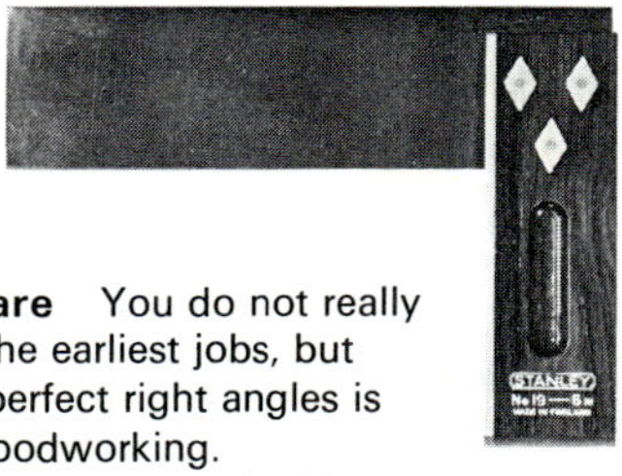

Trysquare or **Setsquare** You do not really *need* one of these for the earliest jobs, but marking out timber in perfect right angles is an important part of woodworking. Therefore it is as well to get one early. Since this is, like the spirit level, a tool without a cutting edge, one *can* economise on it. Cheap ones are usually reasonably accurate, though they may be more easily knocked out of true than dear ones.

Sandpaper

You will also need a few sheets of sandpaper for smoothing off. This is made in different grades of roughness. Buy No. 2 Medium for the first smoothing and No. 0 Fine for finishing off.

Rawlplugs

One especially useful tool, if you intend to fix shelves to solid walls, is a Rawlplug Hammer Drill, and of course a supply of Rawlplugs. These provide the simplest and quickest way of making a strong attachment to a wall. You can buy them in small sets, complete with drill, plugs and screws.

Introduction

Woodwork for the home calls for cutting wood to shape, smoothing it and joining the parts together. There is nothing very difficult in any of these operations. A highly skilled woodworker might do the jobs quicker and more accurately but for all normal domestic purposes anyone can easily learn to use wood.

Most furniture is made up of shelves, frames and boxes of different sizes. A kitchen wall unit may be a simple open shelf, or a box with a shelf inside. Drawers are only boxes shaped to fit inside other boxes. Fit legs to a box and you have a dressing table. Make a very tall box and you have a wardrobe. Four legs held together by a rail near the top is the basis of a stool (with a padded top), or a table (with a solid wooden top). Lengthen the back legs upwards and add a cross-piece to make a chair.

Wood is bought in strips, planks or sheets. All are cut and smoothed in much the same manner. Only the ways in which they are joined together are different. By learning to make a few simple basic joints and structures you can soon make almost any article used in the home.

The plan of this book is simple.

First we look at tools. There is no need to buy a great number of these. The first items we describe are made with no more than a hammer, saw and screwdriver. Later you can add other tools for special jobs.

As wood is the basic raw material we also take a look at the way in which it is bought, and the different kinds available.

The working sections then begin with the making of the most useful and universal of all home woodwork jobs—a shelf. Just a simple shelf attached to a wall. Then we take a step forward to make the simplest of all woodworking joints, the butt joint, and show how to build a range of simple shelf groups.

By adding doors and a back to a shelf set we can make a wall-unit for the kitchen, and this is followed by a larger set of free-standing shelves for books, using housing joints.

Each project is arranged to show the use of some new joint or process, and one or two more tools, progressing gradually to the more difficult joints such as the dovetail joint used in drawers.

By working through the book, anyone who has never made anything in wood before will be able to construct more and more useful and attractive furnishings, and also be able to make up individual designs.

Everyone needs shelves. Most of us like them in sets. Every kitchen calls for units of cupboards and drawers, some with hard-wearing working surfaces, with sliding or hinged doors, or supporting a sink. Most of us would like a coffee table, extra dining chairs, chests of drawers, built-in wardrobes and fitted dressing tables. By making them at home we can save money and the furniture will be exactly the right size and shape for our home. Often too, we can afford to buy wood of a quality found only in the dearest furniture, because of the saving we make in 'doing it ourselves'.

Nor need the furniture look 'home made'. Given time and patience anyone can produce work as accurate as any made in a factory. And there are plenty of ancient tricks of the trade to correct those errors which all of us make at times!

This is a book for the workbench or table. Not a book to be read, but followed. A book to have open at your side, covered in sawdust, perhaps, as the job is being done.

Only practice and care can make a skilled woodworker, but we hope that those who follow our step-by-step pictures will realise that the road is not so difficult—and really very rewarding.

Section One

A word about wood

There are two main types of wood, *hardwoods* and *softwoods*. With a few exceptions, hardwoods are expensive, attractive in appearance, more difficult than usual to shape and smooth, wear well and take a lovely polish. Many varieties are not available in long lengths.

Softwoods are often cheaper. They are easy to cut and smooth, and are obtainable in long straight lengths. They may still be attractive in surface finish, and are of course very suitable for work which is to be painted.

All the wood shown in this book is softwood, but any item could be made equally well in hardwood. It is best, though, to start with the cheaper woods, which are also much easier to work with.

All wood contains moisture. A newly felled tree contains a great deal. As the wood is sawn into lengths the water gradually evaporates and the wood shrinks. This process goes on until the wood contains the same percentage of moisture as its surroundings. Obviously, timber left out in the rain will remain damp, whereas timber stored under cover, with freely circulating air, will become dry.

This drying and shrinking is called 'seasoning'. Ideally, it should be continued till the wood contains about 10% moisture. At this point most of the shrinkage will be completed. The wood is now 'seasoned' and can be used for woodwork.

Clearly, if the wood used in furniture were not fully seasoned, and the various parts kept shrinking after assembly, the piece would soon look in a sorry state. It is therefore important to get properly seasoned wood.

Simple inspection cannot tell whether the seasoning is complete or not. Buy from a recognised firm of wood dealers who store their timber in neat stacks under cover, in open-sided racks. Do not buy wood that has been standing outside, even if only for a few days.

Incidentally, *age* as such has little to do with seasoning. A very old length of wood, quite dark with age, may be totally unseasoned in the real sense, whereas a fresh-cut plank can be force-dried in specially heated kilns and be fully seasoned in a few hours.

However, even fully seasoned wood will continue to shrink, or else may expand again, if it is taken into an atmosphere drier or damper than its storage place at the timber yard. For this reason, always buy your wood a week or more in advance of need, and store it in the room in which it is finally to stand. Here it will lose or absorb moisture, swell or shrink accordingly, and then remain at that size.

Unfortunately for woodworkers, planks of unseasoned timber do not remain flat after sawing. The shrinkage is not regular throughout the wood. The nearer the wood was to the outer bark of the tree, the more it appears to shrink. This means that if a plank is sawn from the side of a tree trunk, the outer part will shrink more than the inner, pulling the plank into a curve. The only planks which will not curve on seasoning are those cut right across, or towards, the heart of the tree.

The wider the planks, the worse the curve, so one usually avoids having really wide planks—above about seven in. or so. Instead, two planks are glued side by side. If you *must* have a single broad plank, get a well-seasoned one with a grain at the end as in picture D.

Before the days of *plywood* the really large sheets of wood like table tops were all made up of strips of wood glued edge-to-edge. Thin, tough panels such as we now find in wardrobe sides, for example, were impossible to obtain.

Nowadays, though, we can buy really large sheets, 8 ft. long by 4 ft. wide, of plywood or blockboard. Their surfaces look like a continuous sheet of solid timber, but they are really made up of several very thin layers of wood, glued flat together.

In plywood, as many as 32 thicknesses of

wood might be glued together, the grain of each sheet running at right angles to the sheet above and below it. Because of this arrangement, and the extreme thinness of each sheet, the shrinkage of one sheet is opposed by the shrinkage of the sheets above and below, so that the plywood as a whole does not warp.

Some ply is faced with decorative hardwood.

For large flat surfaces, then, plywood may be used. The thinner sorts are not very stiff, so they are usually surrounded by a frame of ordinary timber, to which the ply is glued, or in which slots are cut to hold the ply edges.

Blockboard is a rather thicker material, from $\frac{5}{8}$ in. thick upwards, consisting of lengths of timber laid side by side, and sandwiched between two sheets of plywood. The whole lot is strongly glued and makes a thick, non-warping, stiff board which can, in many cases, be used without framing.

Some popular boards are made up from sawdust or chippings, glued together and rolled out in large sheets, from $\frac{1}{8}$ in. thick upwards. These are *hardboard* or the thicker and softer *chipboard*. They are much the cheapest sheet materials and have hundreds of uses in the home. You can buy them already covered with sheet plastic, paint or even metal.

Finally there are many varieties of machined 'mouldings' which are strips of wood already shaped to various sections. The most useful of these is the double-channel tracking moulding with which you can make sliding doors for many home items easily and quickly.

To sum up:

1 Always buy fully seasoned timber from a reputable dealer who has proper storage facilities.

2 Plain timber may be hardwood or softwood; start with the softwood and graduate to hardwood later. Avoid wide planks if possible.

3 Plywood is made up of many thin layers of wood glued together. It is tough, reliable and easy to work but needs framing for strength and is not cheap.

4 Blockboard is strong, stiff, seldom requires framing, but is expensive.

5 Hardboard and chipboard are much cheaper, very serviceable indoors, easy to work and will last for years if not harshly treated. They usually need framing.

6 Mouldings are decorative and the channelling is very useful, but they are fairly expensive.

Buying your materials

There are some things to watch when buying wood. For example, if you order a strip of wood 2 in. by 1 in. in thickness you will not get it. Instead you will be given wood about $1\frac{7}{8}$ in. by $\frac{7}{8}$ in. thick!

There is nothing illegal about this, because it is one of the 'customs of the trade'.

The reason is that all wood measurements start from the bulk tree trunk, *before* it is sawn up. Suppose that a trunk is exactly a foot square.

If the woodyard machinists saw this into 12 equal planks a foot wide, these will not be an inch thick, *because of the wood removed by the saw blade*. Instead they will be thinner than an inch. But it is the trade custom to refer to them as '1 in.' rough-sawn timber. Now suppose that such a plank were cut into six equal strips 2 in. wide. These would not in fact be *exactly* 2 in. across, but a little less.

Further, if these pieces are put through the planing machines to transform them into smooth sided strips such as we would usually buy for our work, even more wood will be planed off, making the pieces still less again than 2 in. by 1 in. But they are still referred to as '2 in. by 1 in.' planed-all-round timber.

In planning any woodwork job then we must take care that we allow for these odd $\frac{1}{8}$ in. of missing thickness. Otherwise we shall end up with parts which will not fit together. This is also why, when making

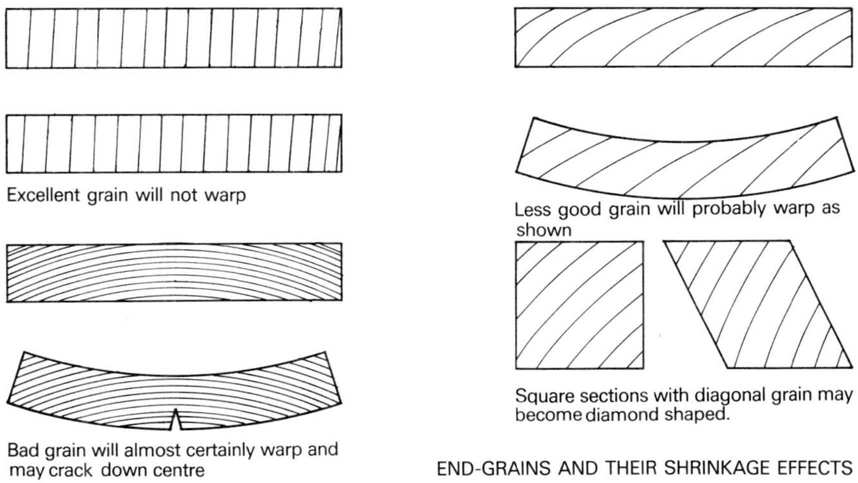

END-GRAINS AND THEIR SHRINKAGE EFFECTS

joints, we must always measure each piece of wood, rather than relying on prearranged sizes. The strips will differ quite a lot from batch to batch.

You can order wood *rough sawn, partly*, or *fully planed* on all sides. For all the projects in our book we have assumed that you will buy fully planed wood. It is quite possible to plane your own timber from rough-sawn wood, but this is a fairly skilled job and takes time. The saving is only pence per foot of wood and is not really worth while.

The best way to buy wood is to find a local timber merchant, with his own machines and large, under-cover stocks of wood. He will have all manner of information about the types of wood stocked in your district, their relative costs and the work they are best suited to.

The men who work in the yards are usually most helpful in advising on the choice of wood, and it is not unknown for the friendly customer to be offered short offcut lengths at a reduced price.

When looking at timber, see if you can pick out planks or strips that have nearly straight grain, without many knots, which are not warped and twisted and whose end grain, as seen from the sawn end of the piece, is good. The diagram above shows the effects of the different end grains on shrinkage and warping. Timber with the best end grain costs more, for technical reasons, to saw out, so it may be dearer; but it is still well worth choosing.

Some shops sell timber for the home woodworker nowadays. They often stock the more expensive and unusual woods—those for which the large scale timber merchant may have little call. You will find the prices at these shops well above the timber yard level, for the shopkeeper must of course make some profit on the sale. However, many owners of such shops are themselves keen and experienced woodworkers, willing to help and advise.

Do-It-Yourself shops like this are most useful for the advanced woodworker seeking better wood. It pays, though, to deal with a merchant when buying softwoods.

Sheet materials are more or less standardised in price at large yards, but merchants will rarely bother to sell part-sheets. You must go to a shop for these. But sheeting so often comes in useful for odd jobs that it is worth while buying in full sheets and keeping what is left over. Incidentally, do not expect the merchant to *deliver* your small order. But if the sheets are big he will always cut them smaller for you to carry away.

In our features to make, we give an indication of *cost* in each case but wood and fittings come in a wide range of sorts and qualities as well as varying in price from place to place. So all costs should be considered as approximate guides only. Make local checks before ordering.

Section Two

1 Using saw and hammer to make simple shelves

Few housewives will admit to having enough shelves. Whether in the kitchen, the pantry, the hall, in the alcoves beside the living-room fire, in the bathroom or bedroom, there seems always to be a need for one more shelf.

Erecting a simple shelf is an ideal practice item.

There are two main types. One is held up by brackets attached to the wall so that the shelf projects from the wall, and the other is fitted into some alcove or corner and is held up by wooden supports at the ends.

The one we show has *both* types of support, and is fitted into a corner of a room. At one end is a simple steel angle bracket, at the other is a wooden cross-support screwed to the adjacent wall.

The position of all the holes must be marked out first, and it pays to take a little time over this.

In fact, in woodwork as a whole, marking out is one place where newcomers often fail. Accurate cutting, shaping and smoothing is no use if it turns out that the original markings were wrong!

The main problem with mounting shelves on walls is to get a good, secure fastening to the brickwork behind the plaster. This is quite a common problem. The simplest solution is to use Rawlplugs.

Rawlplugs are small fibre tubes which are pushed into holes hammered in the wall. The screws for the shelf brackets are turned into these fibre tubes, expanding them so that they grip the hole tightly. The whole operation is very simple and quick, provided the plaster is sound. On older walls you may find difficulty in making neat holes.

The hammer-in type of drill is normally used for Rawlplugs. Place its tip against the wall and tap gently with the hammer. Every few blows, as the tip penetrates the wall, give the drill a quarter turn to prevent it jamming. After each $\frac{1}{4}$ in. of boring, draw the drill out of the hole to allow the plaster powder to fall clear.

A neater way of making holes is to use a special masonry drill in a hand brace, but it is not worth buying a drill just for a small job like this.

Steel brackets come with ready drilled holes. Wooden supports need holes bored for the screws. Here again, a proper drill or brace is the right tool to use, but it is quite possible to make suitable holes in *softwood* with the hammer-type Rawldrill. Place the wood on a piece of waste wood and tap the drill gently through it, turning it frequently. Occasionally the wood splits, but this is no great matter, for the length involved would only cost a penny or so.

Before mounting the brackets, place a screw tip into each Rawlplug tube and give it one or two turns. Then withdraw it. This will cut a kind of 'starting thread' inside the plug and make the mounting easier.

Shelves which are not level look awful, so make several checks with the spirit level. If this is a small tool, check at several different points on the shelf in case minor irregularities in the wood produce a false reading. Also remember to check that the wooden supports are level crossways to the shelf.

Cost

Approximate cost of a shelf and brackets like this: 6s. 0d.

Shelves like these are often fitted in the alcoves beside fireplaces. There is strictly no need in such a case to screw the shelves to their supports. However, this does help to strengthen any weak plugging, so in the early days it is probably best to screw them in completely, as shown in the pictures. In any case, always store fireplace-side shelving in the alcove for a week before erecting it. This will adjust the wood seasoning to suit the warm dry position it will finally occupy.

1 To get the shelf-ends square, first mark across them at an exact right angle. If you have no trysquare yet, the stiff cover of a book will serve quite well. Mark the edges and *both* sides carefully.

2 Place the wood so that it overhangs at the right side of a table or chair. Saw *slowly* across the plank. Sawing without strain takes practice. A sharp saw will need no downward pressure greater than its own weight. Start the cut by drawing the saw towards you, with its teeth *just on the waste side of the marking*. In woodwork, *all* saw cuts are made so that the marking remains visible on the piece being used. Never cut straight down the line itself.

3 To fix a steel bracket shelf, place the first bracket against the wall at the desired height. Then mark the position of all the screw-holes with a pencil.

4 The Rawldrill is a simple means of making a hole in plaster, brick and concrete walls. Tap the drill into the wall, turning it at

2

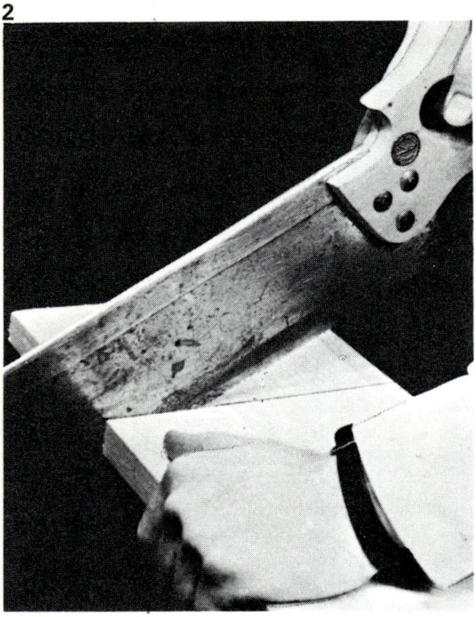

3

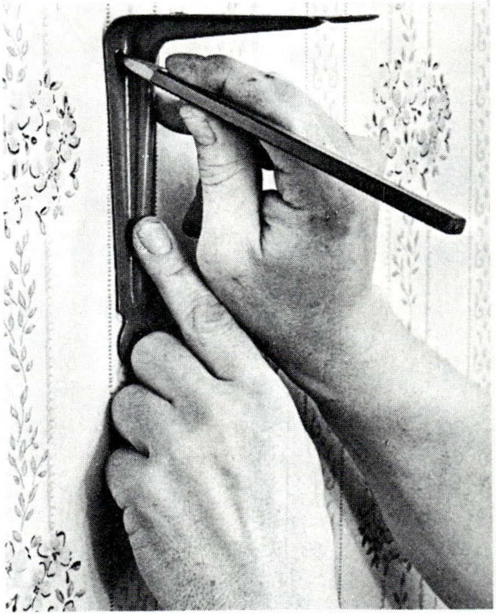

4

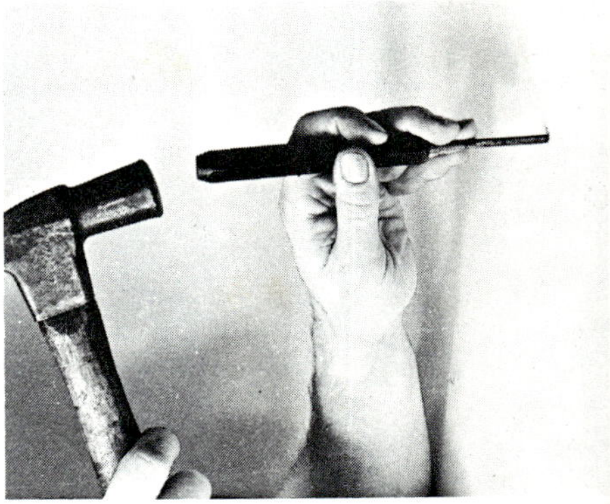

intervals to prevent it jamming and to clear away dust.

5 Push Rawlplugs of the required length into the holes and pass screws through the bracket and into the plugs. It helps to make a start with a screw in every Rawlplug before applying the bracket.

6 Before fixing the second bracket, lay the shelf temporarily in place and get it perfectly level. Mark underneath it with a pencil line along the wall.

5

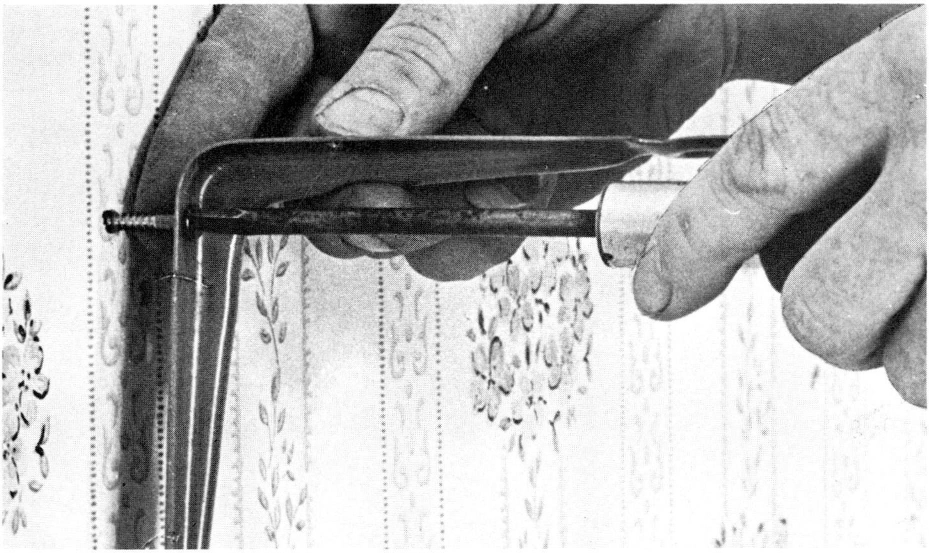

6

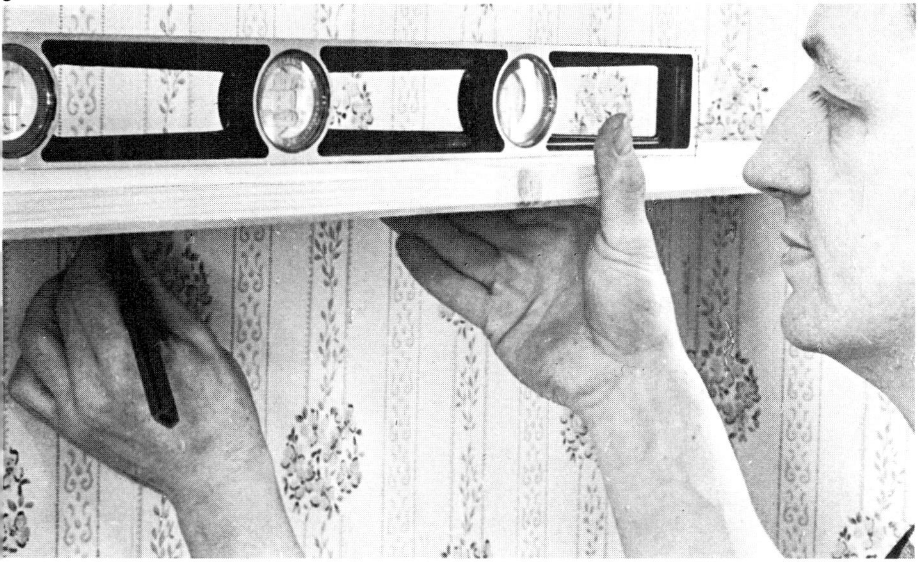

7 The other end of this shelf is arranged in the corner of the room, supported on a wooden length screwed to the wall at the correct height. In alcoves you can use two wooden supports like this, one at each end. Drill holes through the wood for the screws, you can use the Rawldrill, and then pass a marker point through the holes to give the exact positions on the wall for the Rawlplugs.

8 Steel brackets are screwed from the underside. Use countersunk-head screws (see p. 91) a little shorter than the thickness of the shelf.

7

8

9 On wooden supports the shelf is held by longer, thin screws passed downwards through the shelf. As with all screwing it is best to make a hole through the shelf first. Any tightness in the shelf-hole will only weaken the joint.
10 The completed shelf combines the simple wall bracket with the wooden support suited to alcoves. The bracket end has been cut off at an angle to reduce the rather stark 'squareness' of the shelf.

You can buy flat steel brackets for smaller shelves and these may be sunk *into* the plaster beneath the wallpaper, giving an invisible support. Most shelf-supports can be improved by a covering of matching wallpaper.

9

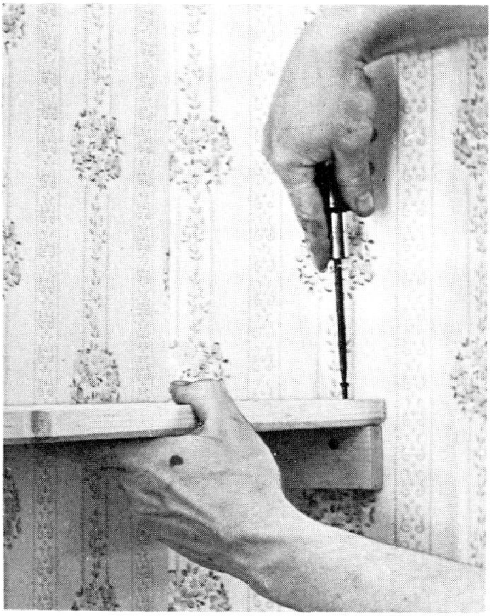

10

2 More uses for simple shelves

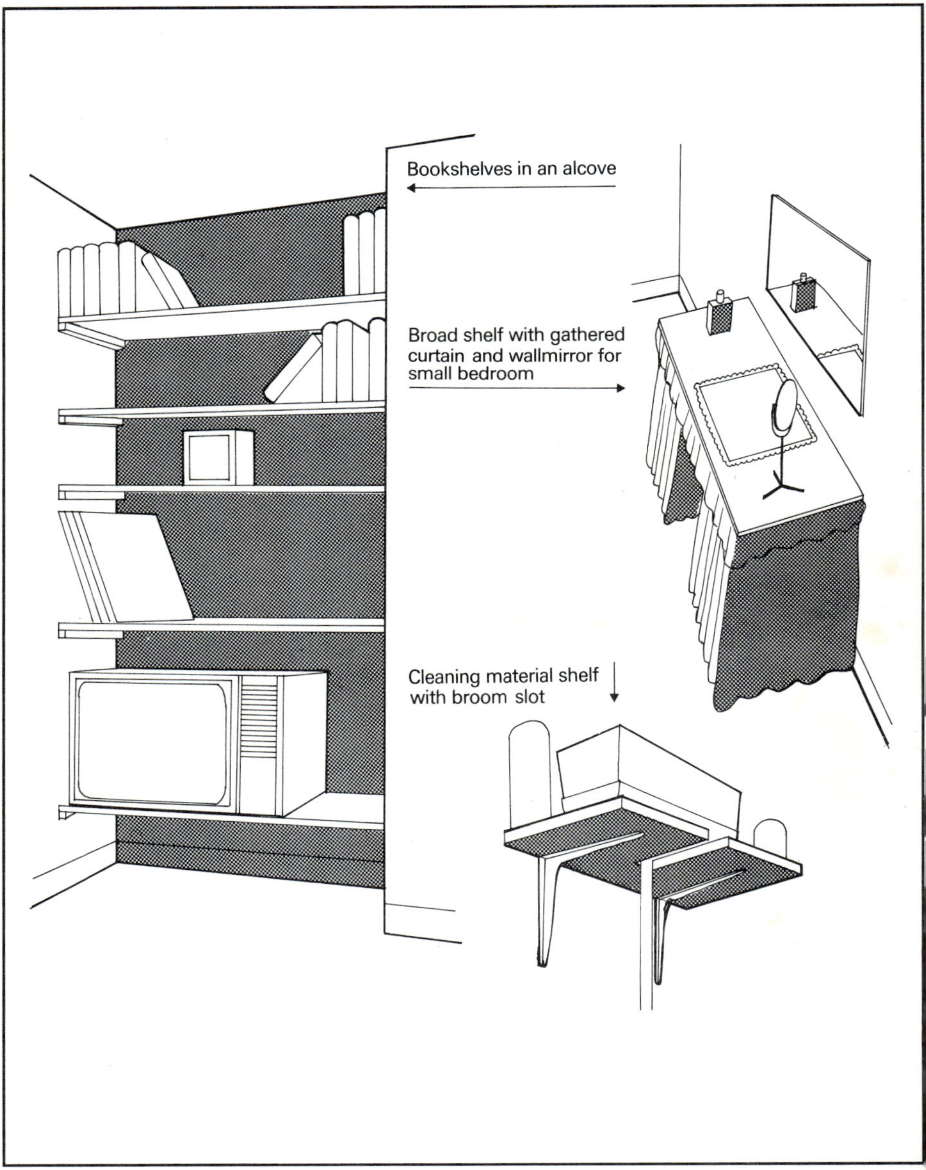

3 Using the butt joint to make a shelf set for the wall

When two flat-edged strips of wood are placed together the result is a butt joint.

This is the simplest of all woodworking joints to make, but unfortunately it is far from strong. Glue has little holding power owing to the small area of contact and the difficulty of making a close butt, so you must add screws and nails to give extra strength.

This little shelf unit is very easy to make and you can use almost any odd lengths of wood for it. The size can be anything from a few inches long, perhaps for a bathroom shelf, to two ft. or even more, in heavier wood, for books or kitchenware.

Nothing could be easier to shape, for apart from one end of each piece, which must be a perfect right angle, irregularities do not matter. There is a good deal of scope, too, for artistic developments, as the idea can be extended to multi-shelf units in various designs.

The mounting is on steel shelf brackets screwed to Rawlplugs, as described in our previous section.

Cost

Approximate cost of a shelf set 2 ft. wide, with brackets: 9s. 0d.

1 Take four pieces of wood of the same width and cut a perfectly square end to each piece. Use a trysquare or the back of a book as before. The other ends of the pieces can be rounded by sawing and sandpapering, or they can be cut at an angle. Minor irregularities do not matter.
2 At the joints, drive thin nails through into the squared ends, like this. Slope alternate nails different ways to give a stronger 'dovetail-nailing' effect. Joints made like this are quite strong, and you can further strengthen them by applying glue to the surfaces before nailing. Arrange the four parts in as accurate a rectangle as possible.
3 The shelf-support brackets are screwed underneath the overhanging parts at each end. That is, one under the upper shelf and one under the lower shelf at the other end. If this does not seem strong enough for the weight to be carried, you can add another bracket pair under both shelves.
4 Finally mount the painted shelf unit to the wall exactly as before. These flat steel brackets are easily hidden beneath the wallpaper.

1

2

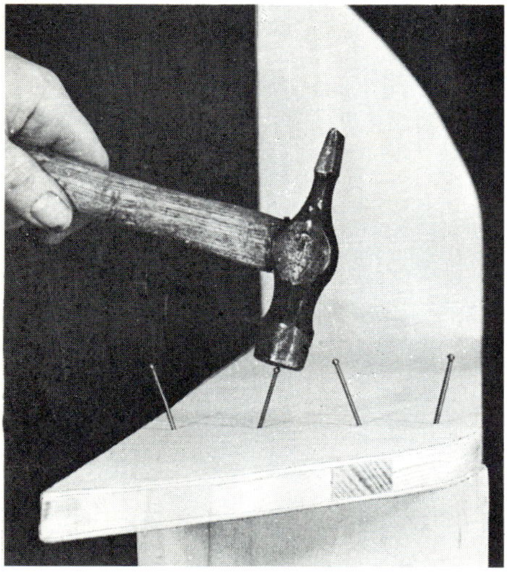

3

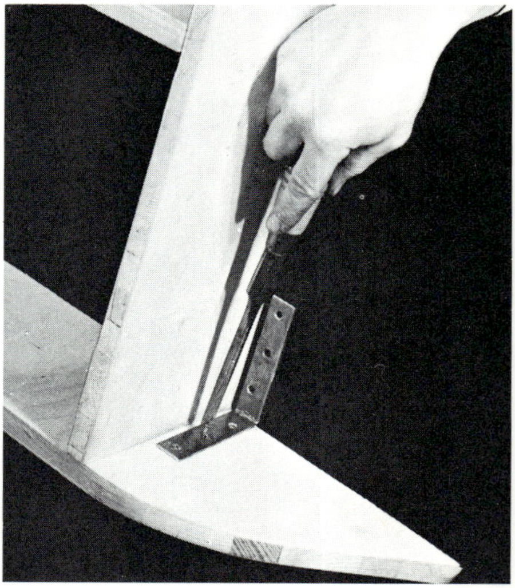

4

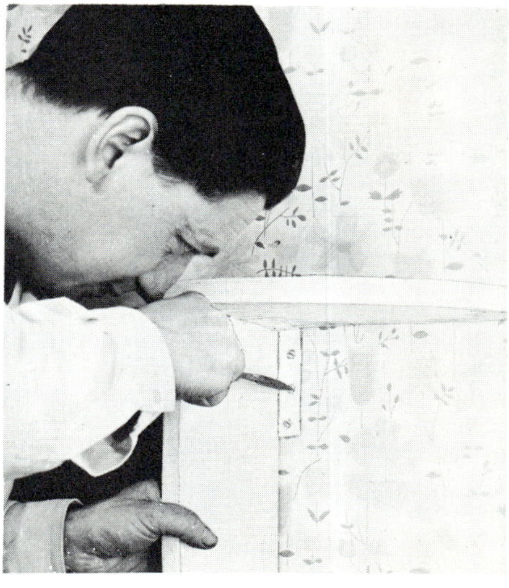

4 Using hardboard and plywood to make a wall cabinet with sliding doors

Cupboards are simply boxes with shelves in them. You can make a wall unit simply by adding a back and doors to an ordinary, butt-jointed set of shelves.

Glueing will be needed for this unit, and the simplest glue to use at first is the plain, liquid glue, brown and sticky, which is sold in tubes ready for use. This does not dry very fast, usually taking overnight, so there is ample time to correct any mistakes before it finally sets.

Plywood is the strongest material to use for the back and doors and need only be $\frac{1}{4}$ in. thick. Hardboard is cheaper, though, and nearly as good for this sort of work where the structure is clear of the floor and not likely to be accidentally damaged.

If you *do* choose hardboard it will need 'conditioning'. This is simply done by wetting the whole of the back (textured) face of the board with plain cold water. About a pint to every 8 by 4 ft. sheet is the recommended dose, but it is not critical. The wetted sheet is then stood for a day in the room it is to occupy. It will swell a little, which will reduce the chance of buckling when the unit is completed.

Large thin sheets must be sawn in a special way. Lay two strips of plain wood about two in. apart on the table or floor. Place the sheet on these with the cutting line over the gap between them. Then use the tenon saw, held nearly horizontal, to cut through the ply or board. In either case, keep the best face of the sheet uppermost. The lower face may well splinter a little along the cut edge. (See illustration.)

For sliding doors it is best to buy ready machined double-channelling. This is made with either deep or shallow channels. The deep channelled type is used for the upper edge, the shallow for the lower. This enables the door sheets to be slid up into the deep upper channels and then lowered into the shallow lower ones. The result is doors which slide easily and which may be removed quickly for cleaning.

Materials

8 in. by 1 in. planed timber, 2 pieces
1 ft. 8 in., 2 pieces 2 ft. 9 in.
7 in. by 1 in. planed timber, 1 piece
2 ft. 9 in.
$\frac{1}{4}$ in. plywood, 1 piece, 1 ft. 8 in. by
2 ft. 11 in. and 2 pieces 1 ft. 4 in. by
1 ft. 6 in. (Hardboard could be used.)
Two oz. panel pins $\frac{3}{4}$ in.
Double channel moulding, 2 pieces 2 ft. 9 in. (one deep, one shallow)
$\frac{1}{2}$ in. sq. oddment wood, 2 pieces 6 in.
4 'Ears' in brass or steel for hanging to wall.
Half pound 2 in. oval nails
Tube of Wood Glue

Cost

Approximate cost 35s., or with hardboard back and doors 30s.

Using Glass for Doors

Glass sliding doors are easily fitted, being installed in the same way as the wooden ones. It is not advisable to try to cut your own glass, as the edges must be ground smooth—not an easy job to tackle at home. You may also need holes drilled to accept the nuts and bolts for handles. This is fairly easy to do with a special glass-cutting bit, held in a geared drill. Surround the hole position with a ring of putty and fill the space with oil when drilling. This will stop overheating of the glass. On the whole, it would probably be best to have this job done too by the glass merchant.

Clear plastic doors are very easy. The material can be sawn neatly with any fine toothed saw, and handles can be glued on. Drilling is done with twist drills.

The disadvantage is the high cost, several shillings a square foot. Another good approach, and cheaper, is to buy surfaced hardboard or ply, with a patterned plastic finish, or wood veneer.

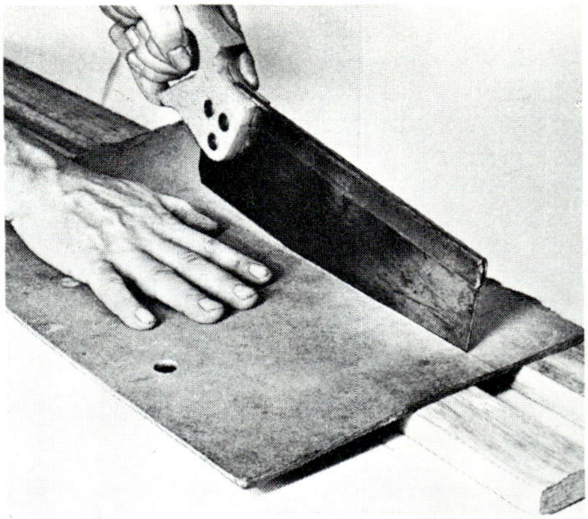

ASSEMBLING THE WALL-CUPBOARD

A 2 sides, planed timber, approx. 8 ins. x1 in. x1 ft. 8 ins. high

B Top and bottom shelves, planed timber 8 ins. x1 x2 ft. 9 ins. long

C Centre shelf, planed timber 7 ins. x1 in. x 2 ft. 9 in long planed timber

D Ply or hardboard back, 1 ft. 8 ins. x 2 ft. 11 ins.

Shelves are dovetail-nailed to sides (middle shelf front is set back 1 in.)

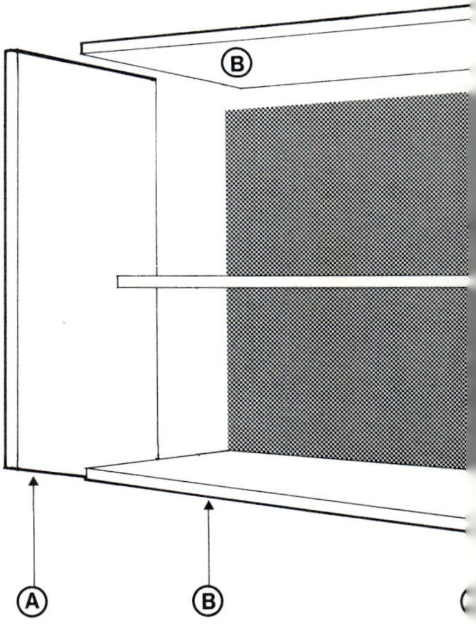

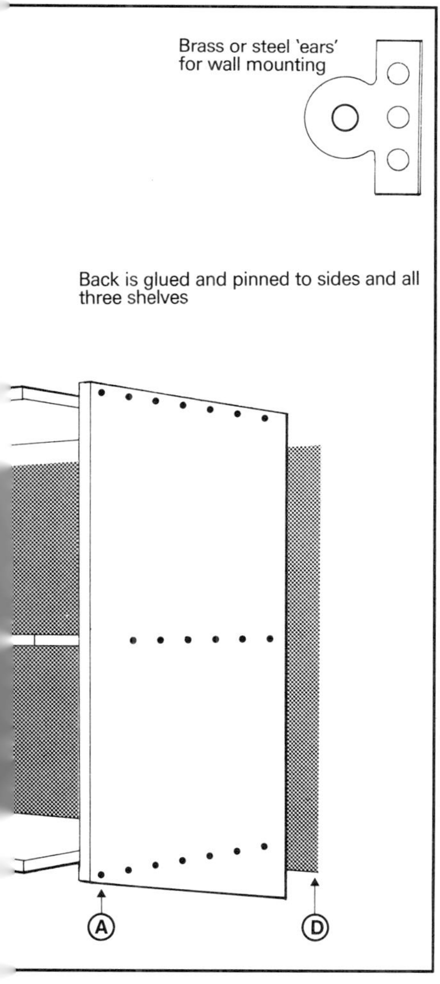

1 When the thin sheets are being fastened into place, the glue should be reinforced by fine nails such as these 'panel pins'. Use them fairly close together. This variety has a pointed-top head which will virtually disappear when driven into the board surface.

It is not easy to hold these tiny pins and drive them without frequent 'hammering of the thumbs'. Get a strip of waste card and push a number of the pins through it . . .

2 . . . then you can hold the pins in place and strike at them with the fingers kept well clear.

Cut three shelves with exactly right-angled ends and all of precisely *the same length*. This is important. They can be made from a single plank of timber if the width is up to 8 in. Try to choose wood with a cross-grain which will not warp (see pp. 11–13). Dovetail-nail the three shelves to two end-pieces of the same material. The centre shelf should be an inch narrower than the others if *sliding* doors are to be fitted.

1

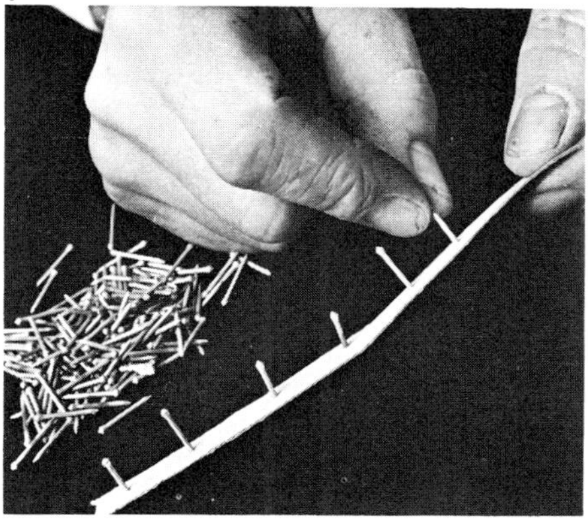

2

3, 4 Cut a length of each type of channelling and glue them to the outer edges of the upper and lower shelves. Remember, the deeper channelling is for the upper shelf. Check that the upper and lower shelves are parallel to each other by carefully measuring the distance between them at both ends and the middle.

Though you can make such wall units without backs, it certainly makes a stronger and more attractive job to nail and glue a sheet of hardboard or ply over the whole back.

5 The doors are simple sheets of board or ply, cut $\frac{1}{2}$ in. taller than the *gap* between the channelling. Handles are simply smoothed pieces of waste wood glued on and secured from behind with panel pins.

Slip the upper edge of each door up into the deep channelling, then let the door drop into the lower, shallow channelling. If necessary, trim the door ends to meet the frame neatly.

6 These units can be mounted with steel brackets, as on p. 18. You can also buy small steel 'ears' to attach to the corners. Drive the screws through the holes into Rawlplugs.

3

5

4

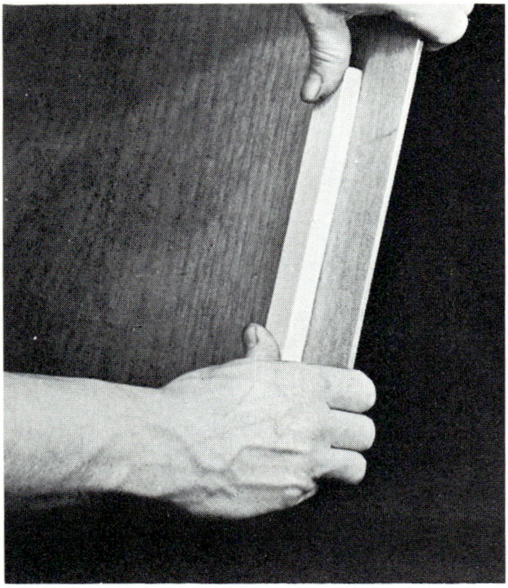

6

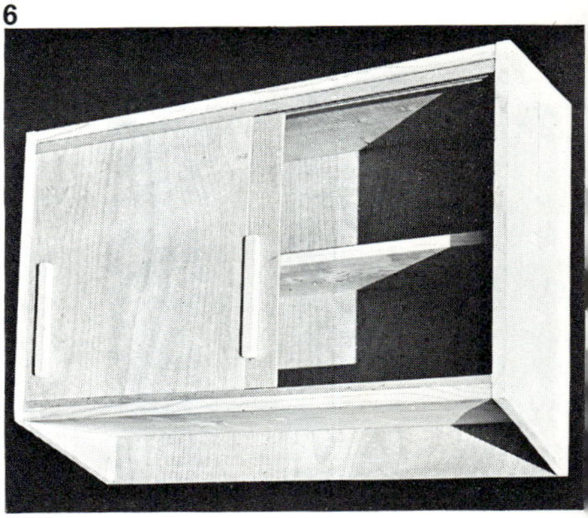

5 Using the housing joint to make a free-standing bookshelf

Bookshelves require a good deal of strength anyway, and if they are not to have the support of a wall, like ordinary shelves, then they must be really rigid and strong.

Ordinary butt joints, even dovetail nailed, will be far too weak for any but the smallest unit. The next step then is to learn about the housing joint, a straightforward but effective means of joining broad planks to each other.

Although well made housing joints may be used to make a unit without a back, the application of a sheet of even the thinnest hardboard so much strengthens the job that it is not worth while to omit it. This will give us the chance to try the modern 'contact adhesives' which are increasingly used in woodwork. They are immensely strong. With some of them, indeed, the wood will tear apart before the glued joints give. But there are difficulties in using them, for once the parts have made contact, it is nearly impossible to separate them again without causing damage.

Tools

To make this unit we shall need, for the first time, a chisel.

Chisels are made in various sizes and shapes, with different names: firmer chisels, bevel-edged chisels, mortice chisels and so on. The professional woodworker, doing many different types of work, prefers to have slightly different tools for specialised jobs. For home use these differences can be ignored. The best all-round chisels to buy are bevel edged, and you will normally need only two; one $\frac{1}{4}$ in. wide and another $\frac{1}{2}$ in. wide.

The quality of the steel is of the utmost importance, for you simply cannot keep a keen edge on poor steel. Two top class chisels are worth a dozen cheap ones.

Firmer chisel with square edges

Bevelled-edge chisel

Traditionally, chisels were made with wooden handles. These could not be hammered or the wood split, so a special wooden mallet had to be used. When buying new chisels now, though, you can get solid, shockproof plastic handles which can be hammered freely and these are by far the most convenient.

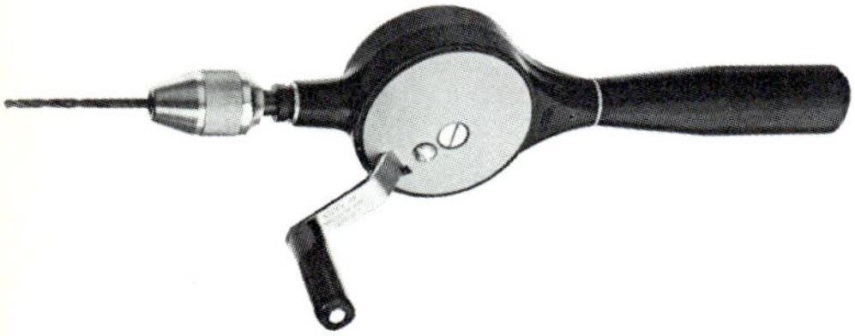

1 You can often improvise helpful tools such as this wooden **Saw-cut guide**. Take a piece of wood, roughly 2 in. by 1 in. across and 1 ft. long. To one end of this nail another, much shorter piece which has had its end cut off at a sharp angle.

2 Place the home-made sawing guide on the edge line, with the pointed end firmly against the edge of the timber.

Drill

There are two tools for boring holes in wood. The brace and the hand drill. A brace is used solely in woodwork whereas a drill is also used in metalwork and wall drilling. In general, a hand drill is best for small holes. A brace is best for larger holes needed in later projects.

Materials

7 in. by 1 in. planed timber, 4 pieces 3 ft. long, and 2 pieces 4 ft. 6 in. long
$\frac{1}{4}$ in. plywood 4 ft. 6 in. by 3 ft.
(Trimming of shelf ends to square should reduce their length to about 2 ft. 10 in.)
24 countersunk head woodscrews steel no. 8, $2\frac{1}{2}$ in. long
Half pound 1 in. round head nails
Tube or tin of 'Impact Adhesive'
Tube of Wood Glue

Cost

Approximate cost 52s.

It would be easy to fit sliding doors, as in the previous section, to the lower two shelves to make a combined cupboard and shelf unit. In fact the permutations are endless, as the sketches showing possible developments show.

To make a housing joint, cut 'trenches' across the vertical supports, wide enough to accept the ends of the shelves firmly. Carefully mark out, using a trysquare to get the markings at right angles, the whole of the 'trench'. It should be just a fraction narrower than the thickness of the shelf wood, and about $\frac{1}{4}$ in. deep.

As in all cases, it is best to *shade with a pencil the waste wood which is to be cut away*. It is surprising how often you can cheerfully hack away into the wood on the wrong side of the guide lines.

1

2

3 Lay the tenon saw against the guide and draw it gently along the surface to start a cut just on the *waste* side of the line. Saw gently and steadily, holding the guide firmly in the left hand and keeping the tenon saw perfectly vertical. The guide helps with this too.

4 Cut down the necessary depth on both sides of the housing trench and then slide a chisel inwards to take out the waste. Work from the ends of the housing towards the middle. If you try to drive the chisel clean across from side to side you will certainly splinter the further end. Take small pieces at a time. It should *not* be necessary to use a hammer for this sort of job.

5 You will not always want the housing to extend right across the support timber, so the housing must be 'stopped' some distance from the front edge. Mark the housing trench position as before and then use your widest chisel to dig down $\frac{1}{4}$ in. all round the end of it.

3

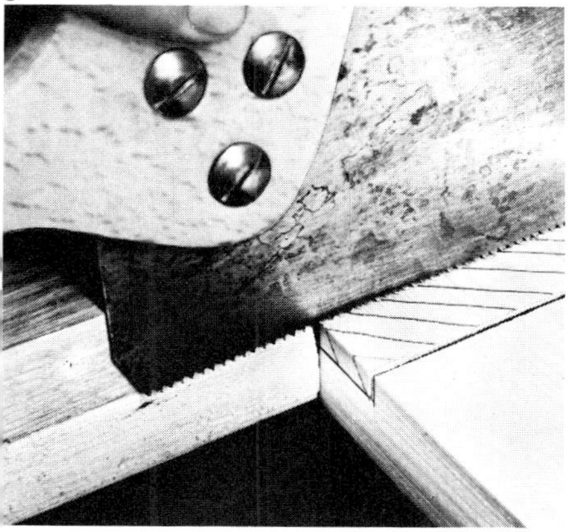

4

5

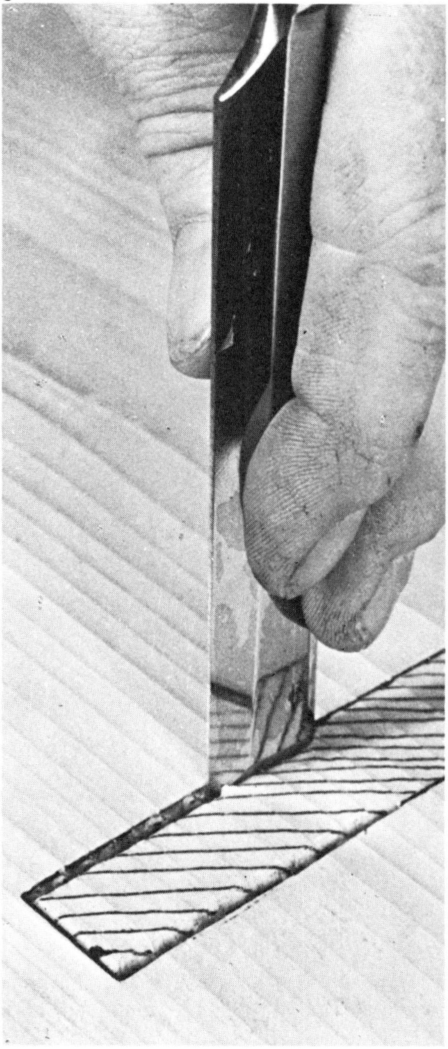

6 Turn the chisel bevel-end downwards and scoop out the wood at the housing end. Keep both hands *behind* the cutting edge at all times.

7 Saw gently down the side-lines. The chiselled-out part will give your saw-tip space to move freely. You can use the sawing guide here too, if you wish.

8 Finally the entire bottom of the housing is cleaned out to an even depth with the chisel.

9 The shelves are simply lengths of timber carefully cut square at their ends. It often helps in assembly to use a wood file, if you have one, to shave off a tiny bevel on the upper and lower faces of the shelf. Instead of a file, use sandpaper wrapped round a flat piece of wood.

6

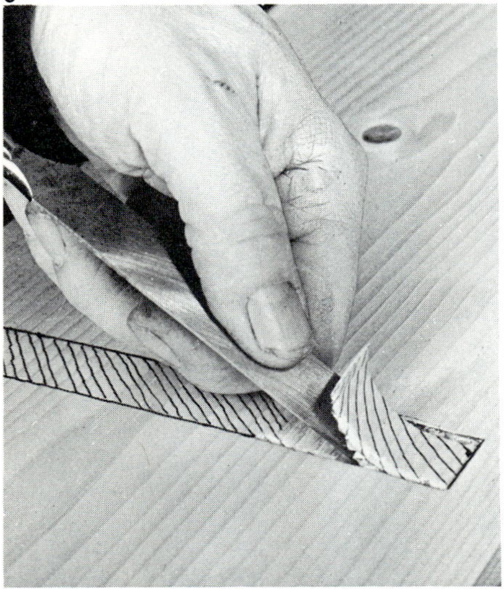

8

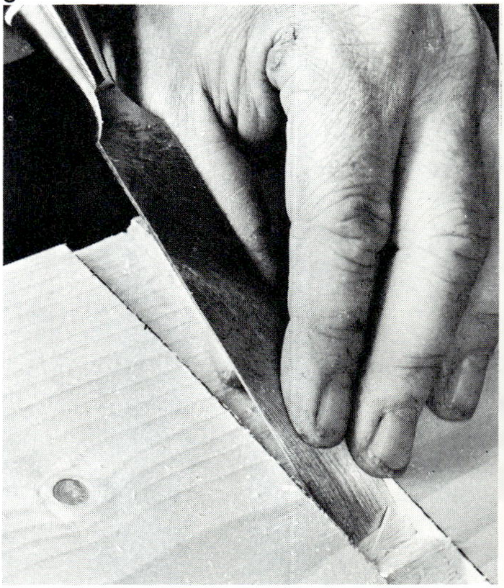

7

9

10 Clean out and adjust the shelves and their housings till they fit snugly. Then bore holes through the support timbers at every housing.

11 Countersunk screws are usually chosen for this job, so use a *countersink cutter* to make proper seatings for the heads.

12 Glue the joints for extra strength with ordinary liquid brown glue and slide each shelf into place. Then drive long, thin screws into the shelf end through the holes. Note that the countersinking is deeper than the screw heads. The space left can be filled up with plastic wood and the screws themselves concealed.

13 Whenever you make framed articles check that they are perfectly square. A simple way of doing this is to take two thin, pointed sticks . . .

10

12

11

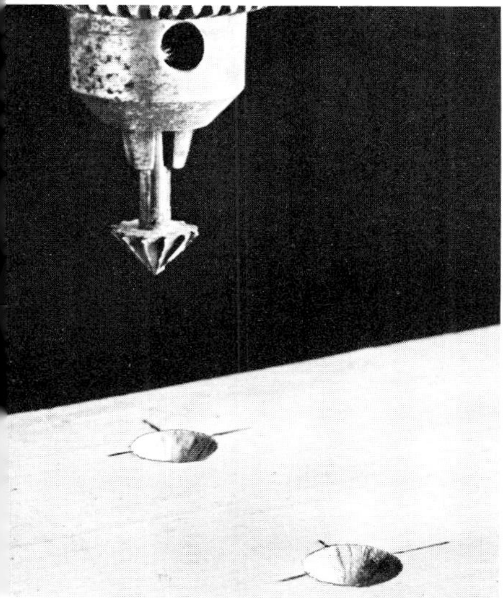

13

14 . . . hold them together till they just fit across the frame from corner to corner.

Pinch the sticks firmly and turn them to lie across the *other* two corners. They should fit exactly. In a true square or rectangle both diagonals are always the same.

15 Another check is to see that the frame is not twisted. Lay two straight strips of wood right over the frame, one at each side, and sight past them from the end. Any twist will be shown up at once by the strips not appearing parallel.

16 'Contact adhesives' are amongst the strongest glues made and have hundreds of uses in home woodwork. Fitting a bookcase back is a good exercise in their use. Because the glue 'grips' instantaneously one *must* get perfect positioning at the first attempt. This calls for some sort of guiding system. Pin oddments of ply or hardboard onto three sides of the frame so that they stick up round where the back is to lie.

17 Study the glue maker's instructions carefully. Some adhesive chemicals are in two parts. Then spread the adhesive over one or both parts of the article being glued.

14

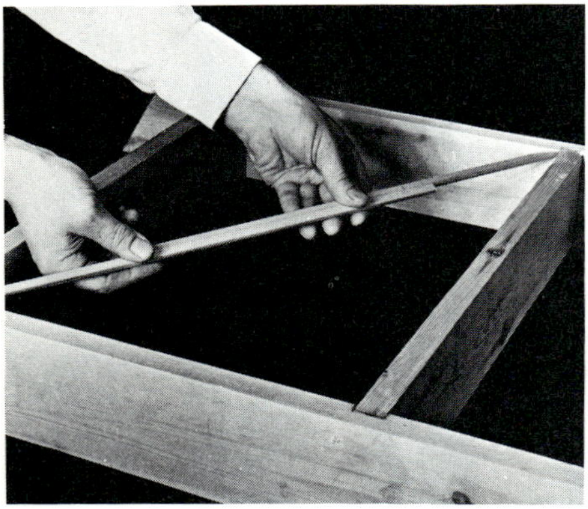

15

16

17

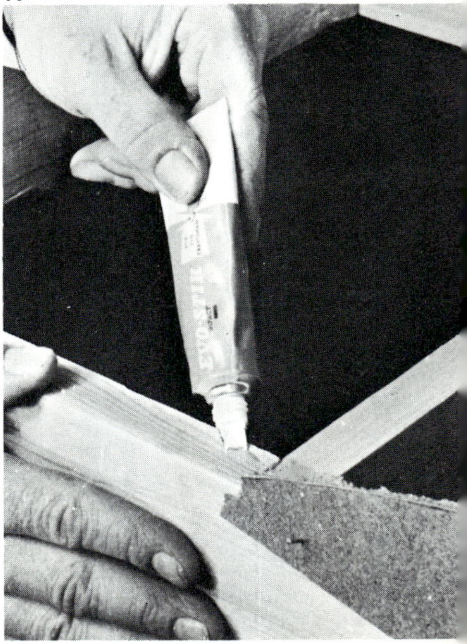

18 Now place the back neatly against the guides at one end of the frame and lower it between the side-guides to meet the frame neatly and accurately all round.

It is usually best to add a few nails or pins. Finally the guides are removed, and any pin marks left are filled with a dab of plastic wood.

19 The shelves of the bookshelf unit are the same width as the uprights, but a small section is cut from their front edges before assembly to fit into the 'stopped' housings. The result is a housing joint which is as neat as a butt joint but much stronger.

20 With the ply back applied, the job is ready for finishing. The top of the back sheet has been slightly shaped to avoid too square an appearance.

18

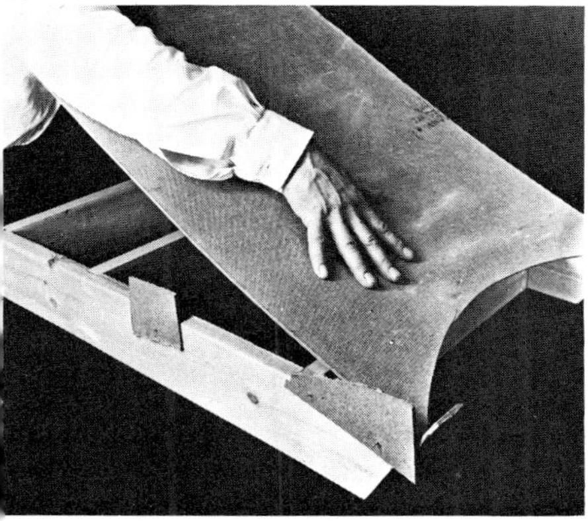

19

20

6 More uses for housing joints and butt joints

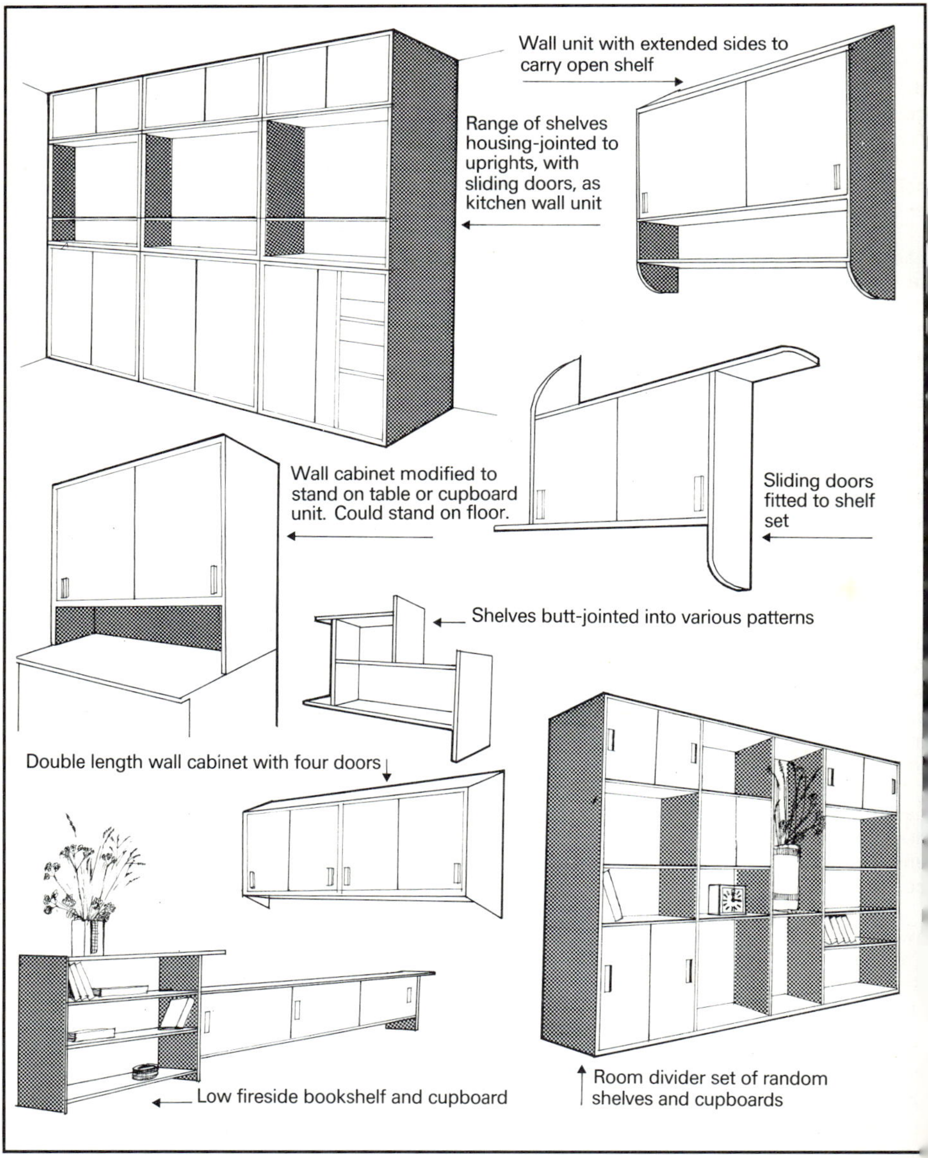

7 Using the half-lap joint and mitre joint to make a kitchen cupboard unit

Kitchen cupboard units with a hard, washable working surface are most popular in all homes and quite easy to make. Here for the first time we meet the wooden frame, covered with thinner sheets of hardboard or ply, to make both sides and back.

As the working surfaces have to bear considerable pressure, we will probably choose blockboard.

In fact, we could use blockboard for all the parts, sides, back and door included, but the result would be very heavy and expensive. By using a concealed frame of thin timber and applied sheeting, we can cut both weight and cost and still produce a fine appearance.

Units can be made in practically any size. Basically though, all are simply boxes, just under three ft. tall, with cupboard doors at the front and shelves inside. Our unit is a narrow type, but you can easily double the length, or treble it, or indeed make sets of units side by side to go right round a kitchen. The principle is the same and once you have made this small one there should be no problems with the larger versions.

Sink units are often fitted into the tops of units like this, in place of the blockboard top. After a little practice with the normal kind, it will be quite simple to arrange your work to accept any sink top you may buy. Only do make certain that you have really strong framing for sink supports.

Besides the open shelves you can also have one or more drawers. The 'shell' to hold drawers is exactly the same as an open shelf unit, without the door. The drawers are only boxes, slid onto the shelf supports.

Drawer making is not difficult, but has its own special problems, and we cover these in a section of their own (see p. 76). For a start, then, let us make the simplest small unit with ordinary shelves.

Tools

You will need some new tools for this job.

Marking gauge This is a device for scratching the surface of timber at measured distances from a moveable wooden block.

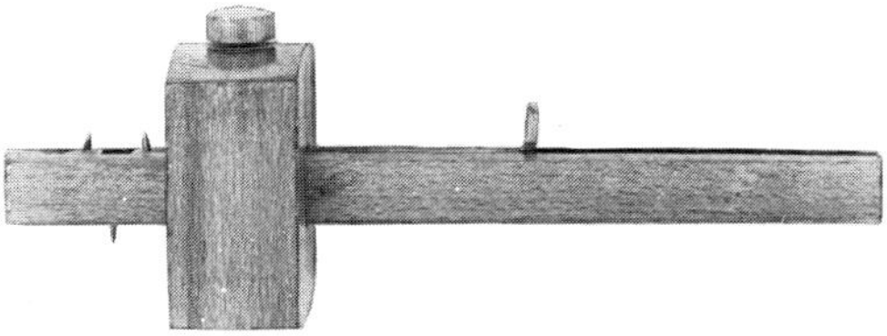

Buy one that has *three* points, one on one side of the wooden handle and two (one moveable) on the other. They are dearer than those gauges with only one point, but they have other uses in more advanced work.

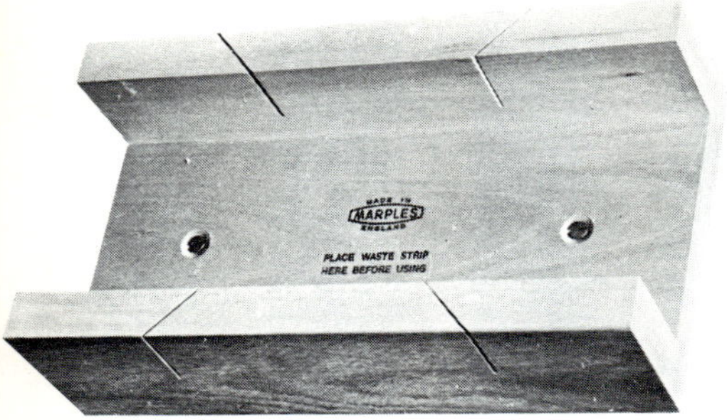

Mitre block or **Mitre box** This is a guide for cutting wood at exactly 45°, half a right angle. The 'block' is L-shaped in section, the 'box' is like a lidless box. Some also have a guide for exact right angle sawing, which is often useful. Buy a good quality one. Cheaper ones in soft wood soon wear, and may warp out of shape.

Surform tool This type of cutter tool has largely replaced the file and rasp for shaping and smoothing of wood. It has handles which adjust to file or plane position, and there are also curved or round cutting blades, enabling many shapes to be cut. It is one of the most useful of all tools for simple woodwork.

Materials

Note. It is suggested that you make this single small unit before attempting any larger version. It is not very costly and the practice will give great confidence in more ambitious work.

2 in. by 1 in. planed timber, 4 pieces
2 ft. 9 in. and 4 pieces 1 ft. 6 in.
4 in. by 1 in. planed timber, 2 pieces
1 ft. 6 in.
1 in. by 1 in. planed timber, 2 pieces
1 ft. 5 in. for each shelf or drawer
$\frac{1}{4}$ in. plywood, 1 ft. 6 in. by 3 ft. 2 in.
$\frac{3}{4}$ in. blockboard, one piece 1 ft. 6 in. by
1 ft. 8 in., and one piece 1 ft. 6 in. by
1 ft. $4\frac{1}{2}$ in.
Hardboard, two pieces 1 ft. 6 in. by
2 ft. 10 in. for side lining, two pieces
1 ft. 6 in. by 3 ft. for outer skin of sides
For doors, either $\frac{3}{4}$ in. blockboard 2 ft. $4\frac{1}{2}$ in.
by 1 ft. 6 in. or
2 in. by 1 in. planed timber, 2 pieces
2 ft. $4\frac{1}{2}$ in. and 2 pieces 1 ft. 6 in.
Hardboard, 2 pieces 2 ft. $4\frac{1}{2}$ in. by 1 ft. 6 in.
8, 2 in. corrugated fasteners
16 countersunk woodscrews no. 6. 1 in.
($\frac{7}{8}$ in. if available)
28 countersunk woodscrews no. 8. 2 in.
4 countersunk woodscrews no. 8. $1\frac{1}{2}$ in.
for each shelf
Wood glue, and contact adhesive
For shelves we recommend $\frac{3}{4}$ in. blockboard
1 ft. $4\frac{1}{2}$ in. by 1 ft. 6 in. each shelf

Cost

Approximate cost without drawers 75s.

1 Another tool which you can make yourself will be handy when sawing timber to length for the framing. This is a 'bench hook'. Get a piece of flat timber, say an inch thick, and about 8 in. by 12 in. to 12 in. by 12 in.

Across one end, nail and screw a strip of 2 in. by 1 in. wood, to its *lower* side.

Across the other end, screw a strip of wood to the *top* side. This piece should be an inch or two shorter than the width of the board, and be so screwed that it does not reach the right-hand edge of the board.

2 To use the bench hook, place it over the edge of a bench or table, with the lower strip firmly against the table edge. Place the wood to be cut against the rear strip, holding it with the left hand. Then saw through it, placing the saw over the gap at the end of the strip.

So, when the saw cuts through, it strikes the baseboard of the bench hook and *not* the table!

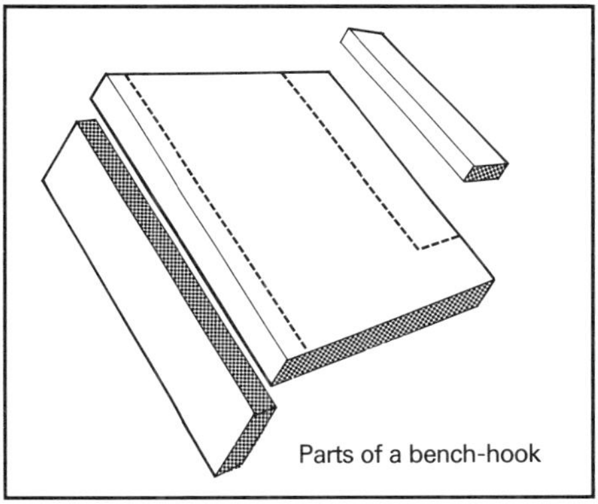

Parts of a bench-hook

2

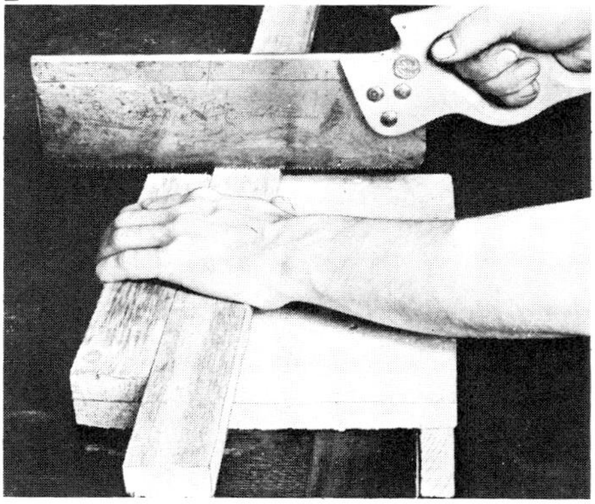

1

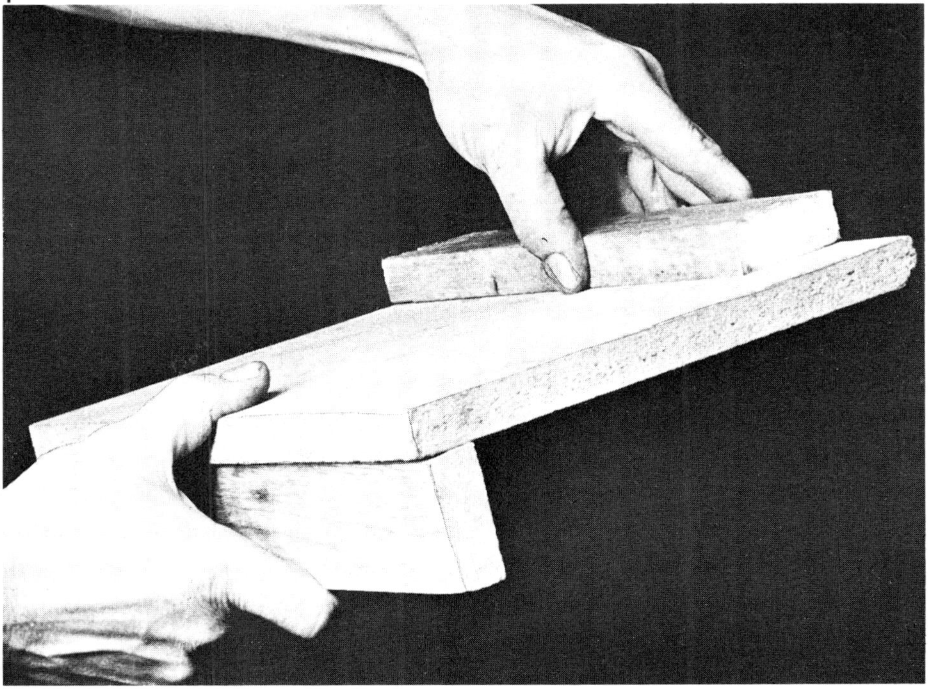

3 Careful marking out and sawing is essential when making the half-lap joint for framing. First use the square to draw a line across one face of the wood.

4 Then continue the line, still using the square, right round the wood till the line meets itself again. This is not quite as simple as it sounds, for the square often slips slightly and the wood itself may not be quite flat. A little practice, though, soon gives the knack.

5 Always make certain that your saw is cutting on the *waste* side of your mark and that the line remains visible on the piece being used.

For simple work like this you can make the lines with pencil or ball-point. Later, for dead accurate fittings, you will use a finely pointed tool to make almost invisible scratches as guides.

6 When two pieces of timber are to be joined at right angles, first place them together as exactly as possible, using a trysquare.

3

5

4

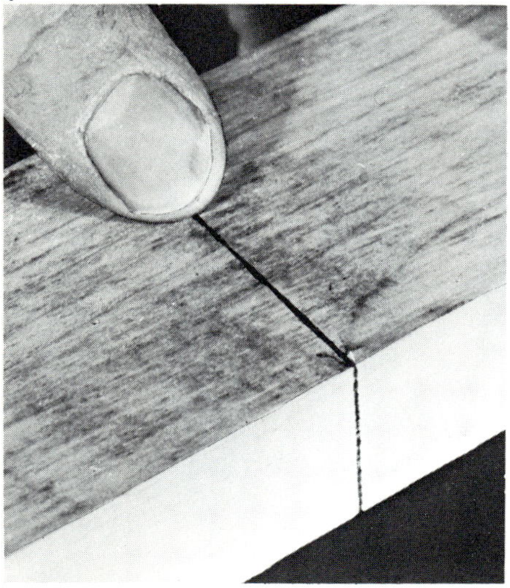

6

7 Hold them firmly together and mark the lower one across its face.
8 Continue this line roughly half way down each side of the strip.
9 Take the marker gauge and set its *single* pin so that it is precisely half the thickness of the wood from the adjustable block.

10 Holding the block firmly against the face of the timber, draw the gauge along to mark a scratch down the centre of the strip on both edges. In marking with a gauge, always use it from the *same face of the piece* on all occasions. You can mark one side of the frame pieces with a pencilled cross to indicate the side you are using. If *all* the parts of the frame are similarly marked it will aid the accuracy of the gauging.

These refinements do little to improve this sort of work, but they become more important as more difficult jobs are tackled.

7

8

9

10

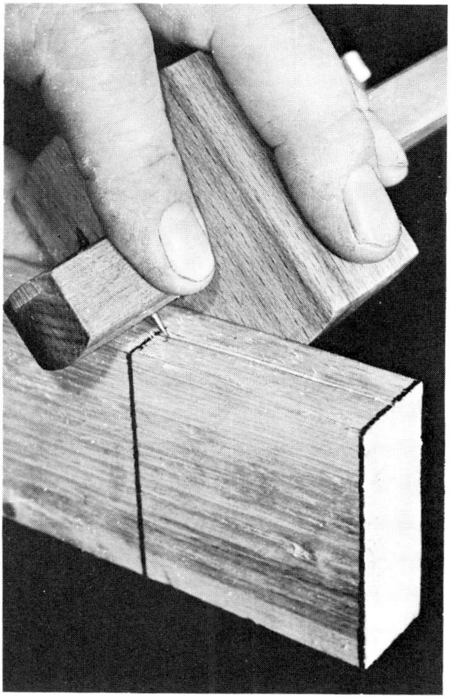

11 Take the tenon saw and cut down on the waste side of the gauge-scratch, but *not* square down through the whole width of the wood. Instead, saw at an angle like this till you reach the full depth. Then saw down at the other side in the same way.
12 Finally finish the cut square down to the bottom. This method will enable you to follow the scratch lines exactly at the edges.
13 Now saw down the cross marking to take off the waste section.

14 Set the waste aside and pare the sawn face of the joint with your broadest chisel, to make it perfectly flat down to the scratch lines.
15 Cut the mating face of the joint in exactly the same way and try the two halves together. Make very fine adjustments with the chisel till they match smoothly and re-check them for square.

11

12

13

14

15

16 Now mark the positions of the screws. These will be about one-third in from the edges and set diagonally to each other. Do *not* place a screw in the outer corners, or the wood may split.

17 Drill, through the upper part only of the joint, a hole large enough to accept the shank of the screw freely. Any tightness here will only weaken the joint. For more details about this see our section on screws and nails, p. 91.

18 If countersunk screws are being used, you can make proper countersinkings for their heads by using the tip of a drill double the previous size, held in the hand and with its shank wrapped in cloth.

19 Spread glue over the joints, following the glue maker's instructions.

20 Finally screw the whole joint together. Do not over-tighten screws in thin wood. In any case, these joints will be much strengthened later by the sheets of hardboard or ply which are to cover them.

16

17

18

19

20

21 The Surform tool can now be used to neaten the ends of the joint. Aim it away from the extreme corner or you may pull splinters from it. Do not press too hard.
22 To join strips in a 'T' position, make one end as before but mark the cross-piece as here, as wide as the strips are broad. Saw down at both ends of your markings and again once or twice in the middle of the waste section. This will greatly ease the removal of the waste by chisel.
23 Start from the edges, as with the housing joint described previously, keeping both hands *well behind* the sharp chisel blade.
24 Finally pare the bottom of the trough flat and smooth to match the end of the joining strip.

21

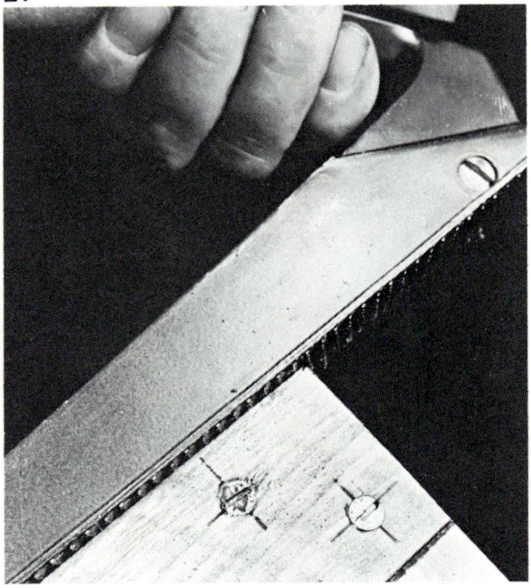

23

22

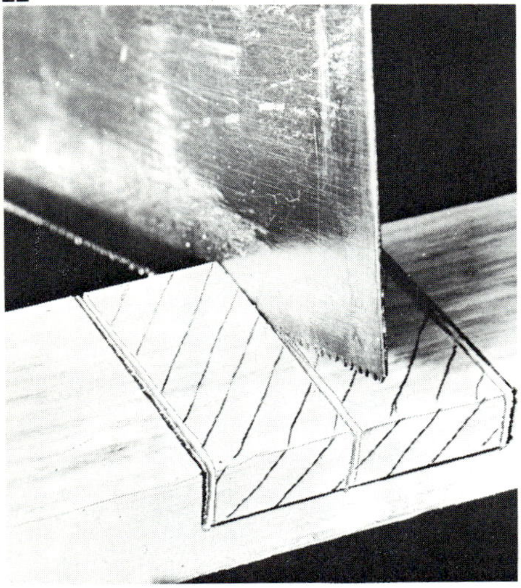

24

We can now start on the building of our unit. The sizes are adjustable to need. This one is 3 ft. tall and 18 in. square.

The blockboard working surface can be covered with plastic sheeting, of which there is a wide variety, ranging from the cheapest oilcloth to glued down, virtually indestructible Formica sheets. Instead of plain hardboard you can use a plastic finished type which will wear a long time and need little maintenance.

THE BASIC FRAME OF THE CUPBOARD UNIT

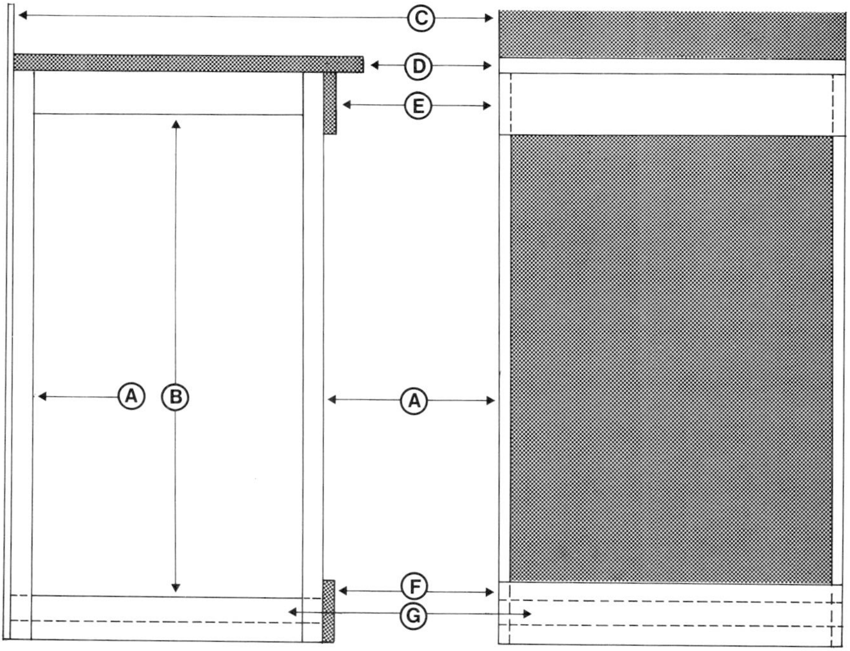

A Verticals (4) of side frame 2 ft. 9 ins. x 2 ins. x 1 in. half-lapped to B

B Cross-pieces (4) of side frame 1 ft. 6 ins. x 2 ins. x 1 in. half-lapped to A

C Back (1) 1 ft. 6 ins. x 3 ft. 2 ins. plywood (¼ in.) nailed and glued to side frames

D Top (1) 1 ft. 6 ins. x 1 ft. 8 ins. x ¾ ins. blockboard screwed to top of side frames

E Upper front rail 1 ft. 6 ins. x 4 ins. x 1 in. screwed to side frames and top

F Lower front rail 1 ft. 6 ins. x 4 ins. x 1 in. screwed to side frames and bottom

G Bottom (1) 1 ft. 6 ins. x 1 ft. 4¼ ins. x ¾ in. blockboard screwed between side frames

Unit is lined and covered at sides with hardboard

25 Make two rectangular frames using half-lap joints in the corners. The wood can be 2 in. by 1 in. in section and the frames are checked for perfect shape as described on pp. 31–2. Cut the back from a single piece of $\frac{1}{4}$ in. plywood. Although you could use hardboard for this, the ply *does* give added strength and is worth the slightly higher cost. Glue and nail it to the two side frames.

26 The top is simply an 18 in. square piece of $\frac{3}{4}$ in. blockboard. Screw this down into the side frames, and nail the back to it too. The front edge overhangs by one inch.

27 The floor is also of blockboard, cut slightly smaller to fit *between* the side frames. Also, its front edge is flush with the front of the side instead of overhanging it. It is positioned 1 in. from the floor.

Sheets of hardboard are sawn out to fit inside the side frames. It would have been possible to do this earlier, when the side frames were made, but it was done this way for photographic reasons.

25

26

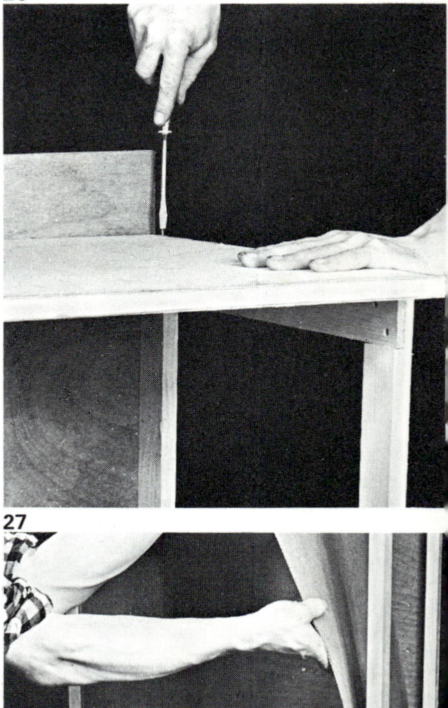

27

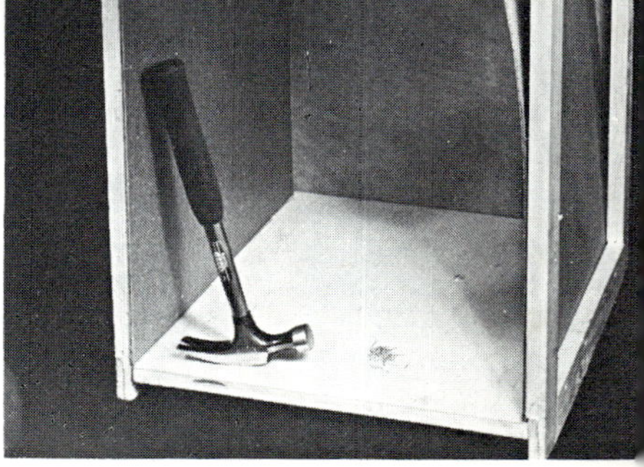

28 Broad strips of straight timber are screwed to the top and bottom front of the frames to give extra rigidity.
29 Finally strips of thinner wood, 1 in. by 1 in. are arranged inside the box at shelf or drawer heights.

Units may be placed side by side, in which case there is no need to cover the outer faces of the sides. But the *ends* must, of course, be covered with a glued-on sheet ready for painting.

30 Shelves can be of solid blockboard, or thin ply with a stiffening piece glued to the front edge. Shelves take a fair amount of wear so blockboard is really best. They do not *have* to be screwed in, but can rest on the side strips. If the job seems too flexible, though, screwing in the shelves may stiffen it up quite a lot.
31 A proper dovetailed drawer can be slid onto similar runners (which must be particularly well attached to the side frames). The drawer is shown being made in a later section. (See p. 76.)

28

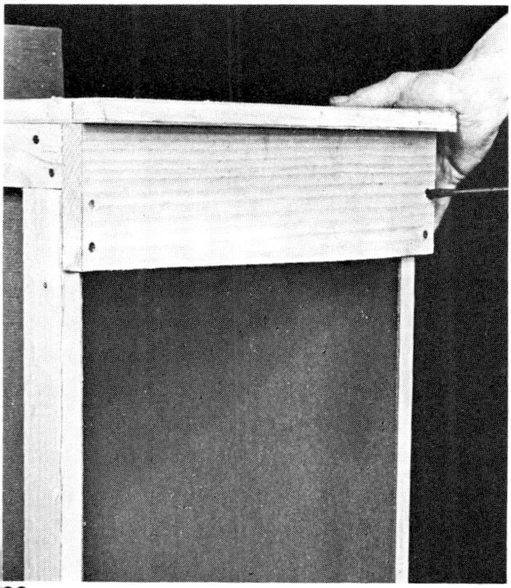

29

30

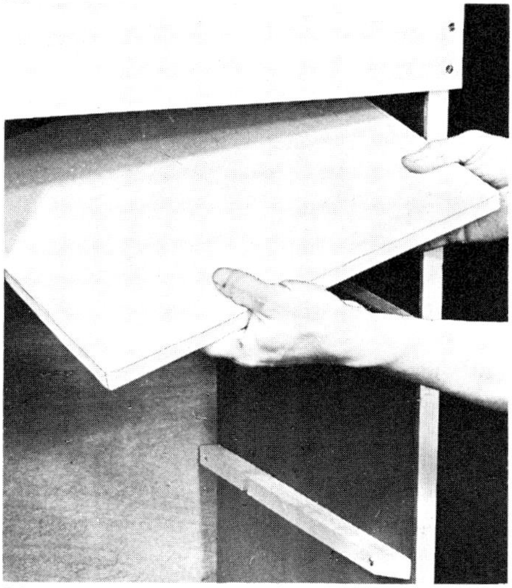

31

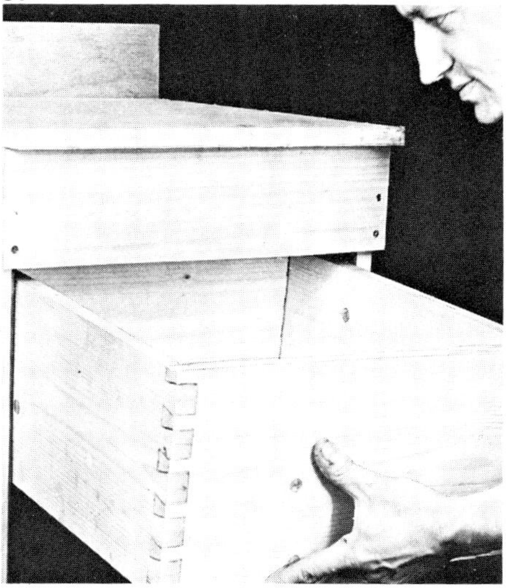

32 A drawer front is then screwed in place from the inside, to fit flush with the unit front. You can fit a whole series of drawers in a unit like this, but you must make the side frames rather stronger and strengthen the back. Drawers are heavy when full.

33 Here is the completed unit, with a hardboard door fitted. A solid blockboard door would be quite suitable and very strong, but it is much cheaper to make the doors from hardboard.

Mitre Joints

Half-lap joints will not do for a neat door, as the joint is visible from the side and does not look attractive. An invisible joint calls for a mitre joint for which we must learn to cut true 45° angles with the mitre box.

1 First, place a strip of waste wood in the box bottom to prevent the saw damaging it.

2 Mark your wood where the mitre cut is to be and place this mark against one of the 45° slots in the box.

32

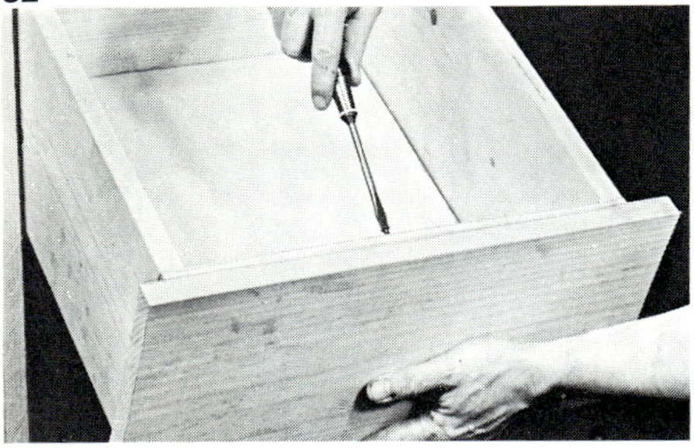

33

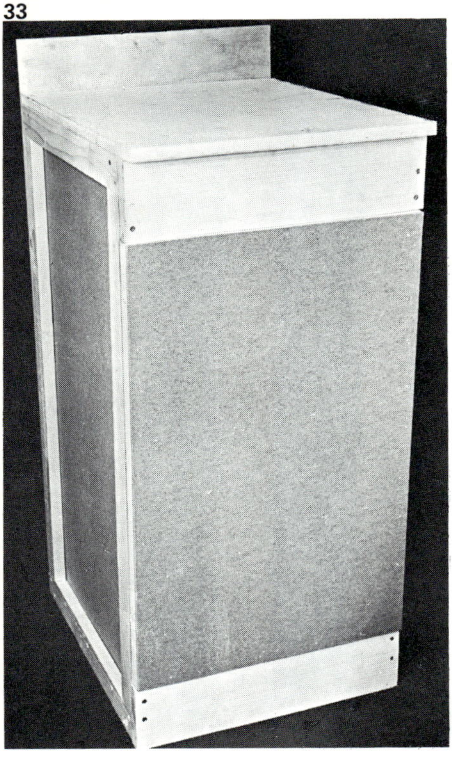

1

2

3 Saw steadily and without pressure down the slots till the wood falls apart.
4 The two parts should fit together to make a perfect right angle.

5 Special jointings are not really necessary for making small doors. Corrugated Fasteners are a useful sort to have though. These are hammered into the wood right across the joint. Their points dig in deeply and the corrugations are arranged to draw the wood parts together.
6 Hardboard doors should be double sided. (Ply is tough enough to need only a single side.) Make a rectangular, mitre-jointed frame and cut the sheet to fit it exactly, or just a little too large.

3

4

5

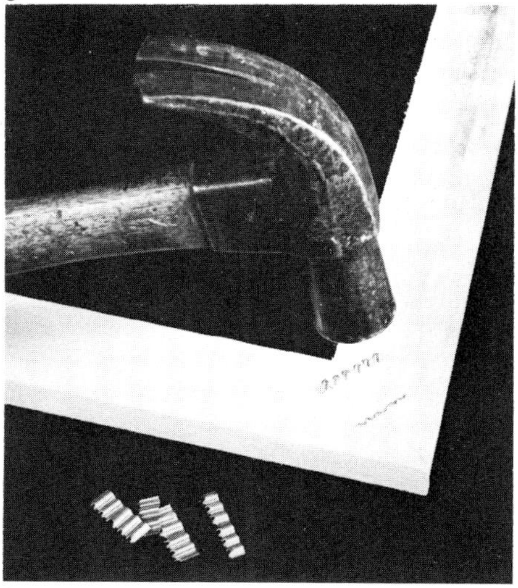

6

7 Glue and pin the sheets to the frame as we did the back of the shelves earlier, using guide pieces if the adhesive is of the strong, 'instant contact' type.
8 Use the Surform tool if you have one, or a very small plane, to neaten and smooth the edges.

9 More details of hinge mounting are given on p. 91 Sheeted doors are easy, because the shape of the hinge can simply be chiselled out of the facing sheet to make a perfect sunk recess for it.

7

8

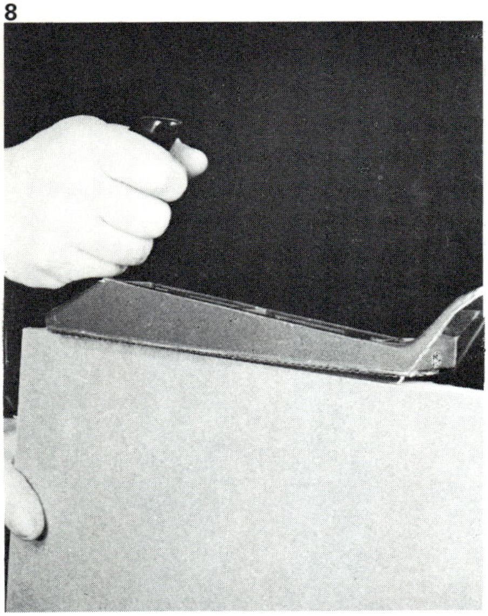

9

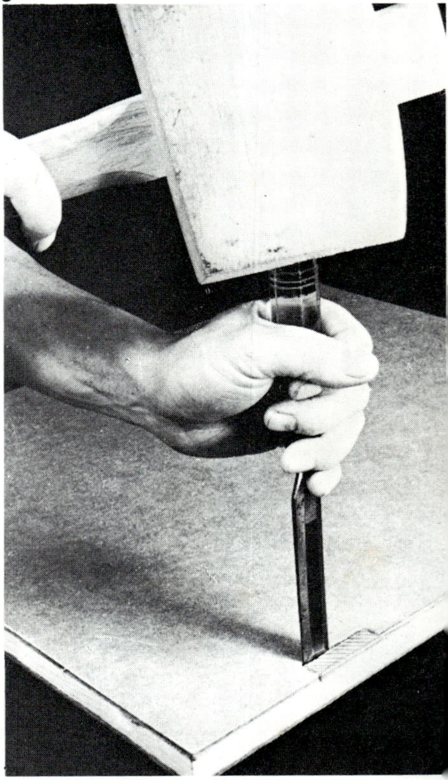

8 Using dowel joints to make a coffee table

In our last project we described the first of the joints used for making open frames in wood, the half-lap joint. Tables and chairs are largely framing, with only the seat or top in sheeting. Although you could use the half-lap joint for such work, it would hardly look elegant and in any case, the half-lap cannot take bending stress very well.

Dowel joints are used for open framing in small tables and some kinds of chairs. They are quick and straightforward to make, and very much stronger than a plain butt joint or half-lap. Since the method is concealed, dowel joints are very neat in appearance from every angle.

Dowels are simply round strips of tough wood, usually bought in yard lengths, from $\frac{1}{4}$ in. diameter to $\frac{1}{2}$ in. or so. They are arranged in place like the screws or nails in butt joints, but the result is much tougher, for the dowels have a large surface area and the glue has a good deal more wood to grip on.

In principle, holes are drilled in each part to be joined, exactly opposite each other. A short length of dowelling is pushed into one hole and then its other end guided into the opposite hole. So the two parts are held together by the dowel.

One dowel alone is rarely used. Two is the minimum, three or four more usual. Therefore it is vital to get all the holes accurately placed. Otherwise the joined parts will not slide together.

Most of the art of dowel jointing consists simply of drilling holes in the correct places. The rest is easy enough.

Besides using dowels to join framing together, you can also use them to fasten planks side by side, as in this table top, for example. As we mentioned in our section on wood, it is difficult to buy really wide planks of solid timber which will not shrink and warp. To make wide planks then, we have to make the edges perfectly straight on several planks and glue them edge-to-edge. It greatly helps this sort of joint to have a few short dowels.

Although we show a coffee table being made, it only needs the addition of a padded top to make it into a long stool. For that matter, one could make the leg section and, instead of the plain wooden top, screw it to the bottom of a box with shelves, like the wall unit on p. 23, and so make a small cabinet on legs for the bedside or lounge. Or the leg framing could be used to support a record player or television set.

One point about the legs, and legs of small furniture in general. One can easily buy ready made legs with screw-on fittings, which can be screwed into place without more ado. These are all very well and are perfectly serviceable. But simple, tapered legs such as we show, take only minutes to make, and would cost, perhaps, sixpence each. A set of ready made legs would certainly cost a great deal more.

In some cases, the cost of commercially made sets and kits is nearly as high as the cost of complete articles. The real saving and interest of home woodwork lies in using the simplest raw materials to best effect, not in fitting kits together at much greater cost.

Moreover, you can often save so much by making the article at home that you can afford to buy solid, first class timber, oak, mahogany, teak and so on. This produces a far better result than cheap wood covered in thin veneer or plastic.

A pleasing softwood to use for this coffee table is Parana pine, which is widely obtainable and not very expensive.

First of all, let us look at the simple, T-shaped dowel joint.

Tools

You will need some more new tools.

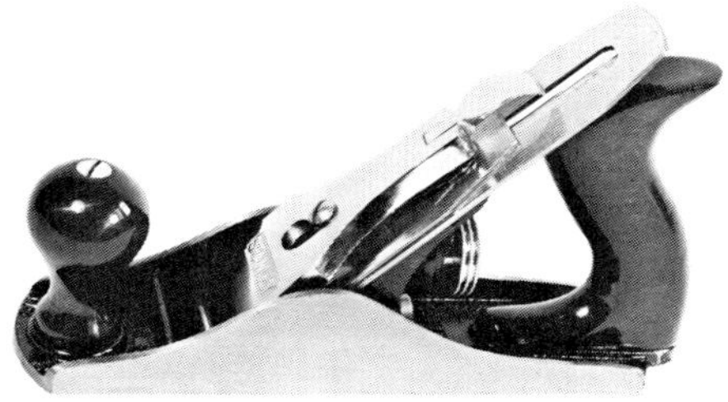

Plane Planes are made in wood or metal. Buy a good metal one. Cheap planes will have poor blades. One roughly 10 in. long is the best all-round size. Keep it in its cardboard box, with the blade wound in, when not in use. A guide to the various settings is nearly always given with each plane. Study it carefully. Note that new planes are *not* fully sharpened but require a final honing to produce a keen edge (see p. 92).

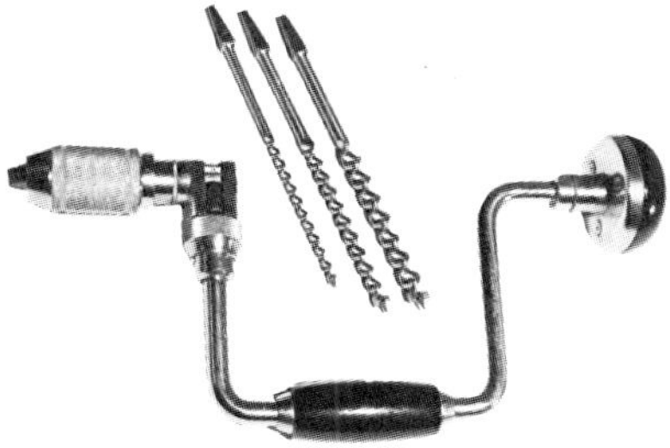

3race Now that we must drill larger holes ve will need a brace and a number of drill its. The types shown are the best for mateur work, being less likely to 'wander' in he holes than others. A brace with a atchet device is best.

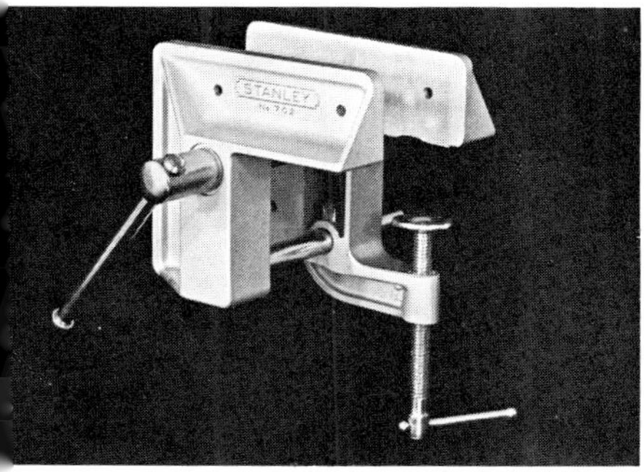

'ice Some means of holding wood firmly vhen it is being worked soon becomes essential. There are many different kinds of vice on the market. For the home worker who has no proper workbench, a vice which clamps onto a table for use as required is probably best. In the long run though, these are not very serviceable and you will probably graduate to the fixed type in due course.

Materials

$7\frac{1}{2}$ in. by 1 in. planed Parana pine, or similar, 2 pieces 3 ft. 6 in. long
3 in. by 1 in. planed Parana pine, 4 pieces 1 ft. 3 in. long
$1\frac{1}{2}$ in. by $1\frac{1}{2}$ in. planed Parana pine, 2 pieces 2 ft. 3 in. and 2 pieces 1 ft. 1 in. long
28 in. $\frac{5}{16}$ in. dowelling
12 countersunk woodscrews brass no. 8, 2 in. long
Wood glue

Cost

Approximate cost 26s.

1 Start with the end of the wood to be joined. Make sure that it is properly squared off. Then draw a line clean down the centre, lengthways.
2 Draw cross lines about $\frac{1}{4}$ in. from each end. This is for two dowel holes. For three or more, simply space the holes out evenly.
3 Tap panel pins into the dead centre positions of the holes, leaving about $\frac{1}{8}$ in. protruding.
4 Now take the cross piece. Mark the position of the joint on its side and press it firmly down into place.
5 Withdraw the wood and the imprint of the pin heads will be clear. The holes in the cross piece are made at exactly these marks.
6 Remove the pins from the other wood strip and bore holes there to take the dowels. The diameter needed will vary with the measurements of the wood being joined. It should not be greater than about a third of the wood's thickness; $\frac{1}{4}$ in., $\frac{5}{16}$ in. and $\frac{3}{8}$ in. are the most usual sizes.

1

2

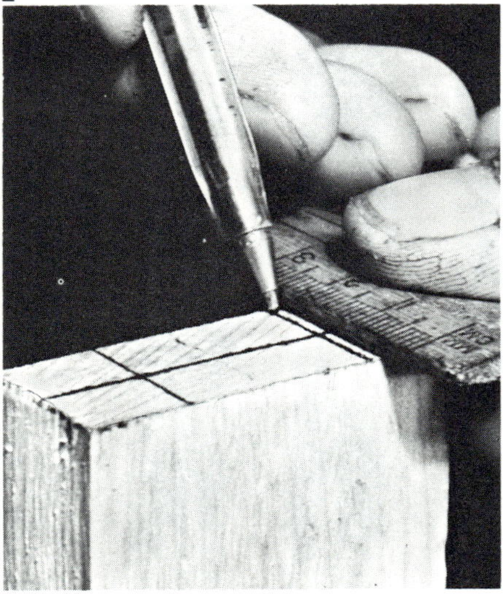

3

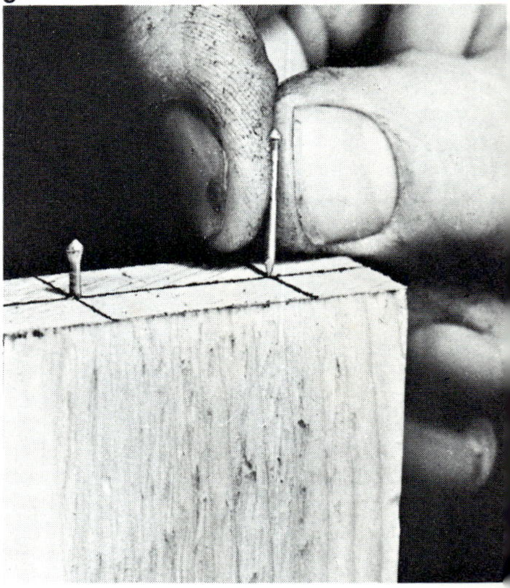

4

If you are using ready-made dowels, try a piece in a hole bored in waste wood, before making your working holes. It sometimes happens that commercial turnings are thinner than their supposed size. If so, then you will have to use a rather smaller drill to make the holes. A firm fit is essential.

7 It helps to run the countersink—or a very much larger drill tip—lightly around the extreme upper edge of the dowel holes. This space will accept any surplus glue forced up past the dowels on assembly.

8 A very light rounding of the dowel tips with file or sandpaper also helps smooth and simple fitting.

5

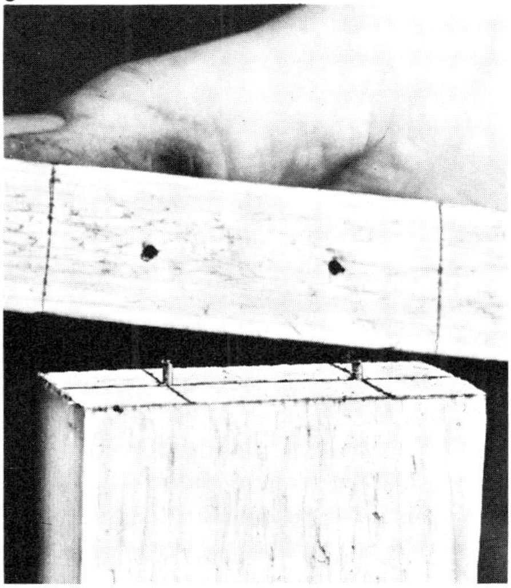

6

7

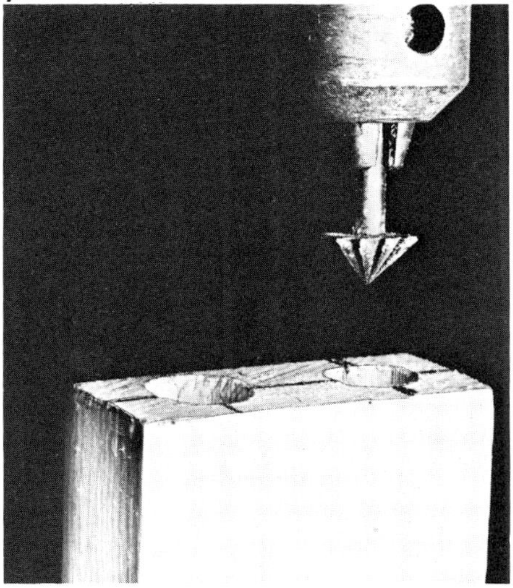

8

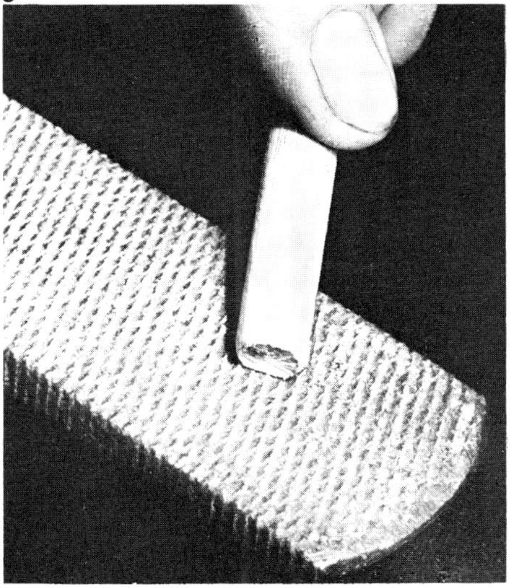

9 Glue trapped below the driven dowels and unable to escape creates many problems. Give it an escape route by sawing a very shallow slot along the length of the dowel with the tenon saw.

10 Spread non-contact type glue over the matching faces of the joint and in the upper parts of the holes.

11 Coat half the dowel with glue and drive it into the holes. Then apply glue to the projecting parts.

12 Mate the cross piece and stem . . .

9

11

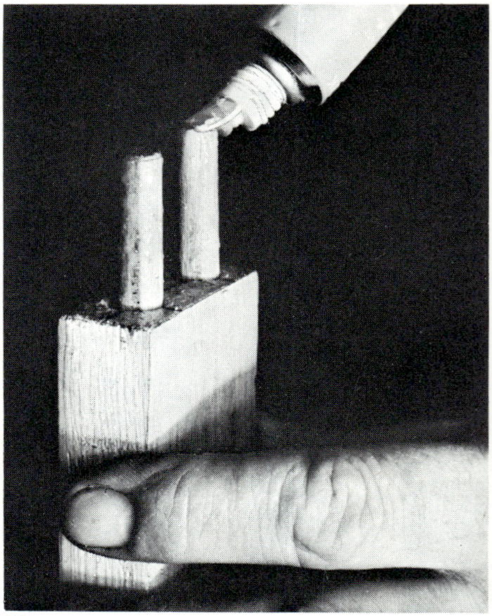

10

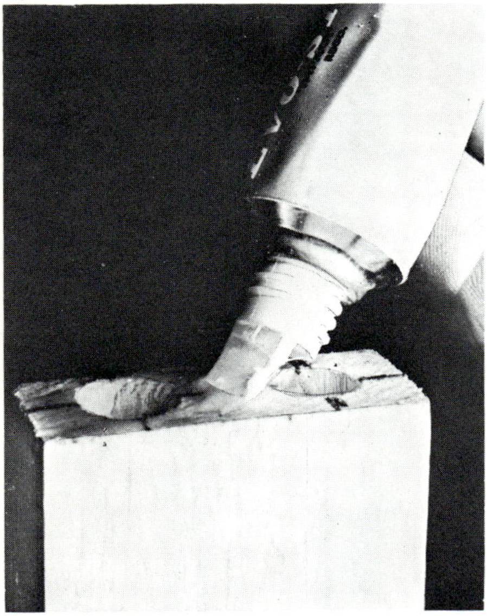

12

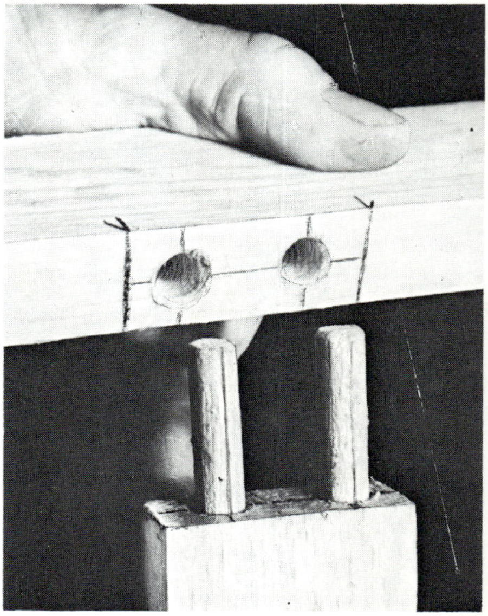

13 . . . and press the parts firmly together. Wipe away any squeezed-out glue *at once*. Glue often stains wood. The joint is now complete and can be set aside to dry.
14 The table top is made by joining two wide planks together. They must, naturally, make a perfect fit along their length. This is one of the more delicate jobs in woodworking and indeed, the matching of really long lengths is a good test of any woodworker's skill. The principle is simple enough. The two parts are clamped tightly together in a vice and the plane is run right along both the edges at once. The longer the plane the better for this work. It also helps to change the planks from side to side, checking frequently for hollows and bulges.

13

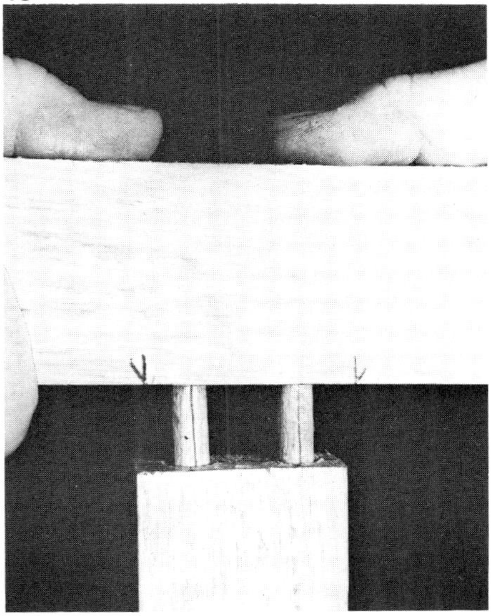

14

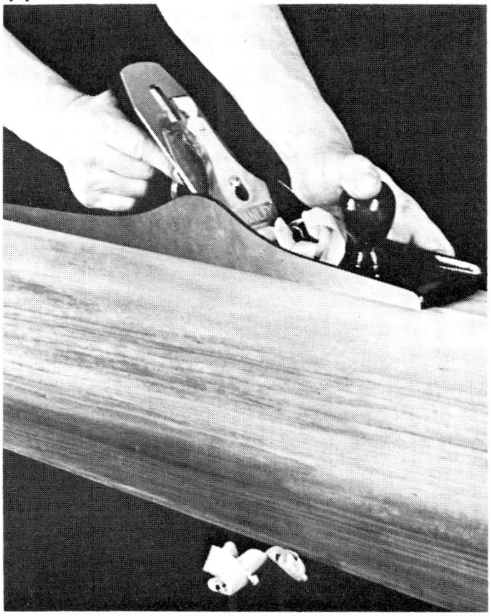

Before starting work on good timber for your table, practice for at least half an hour on odd lengths of wood to get the 'feel' of the plane.

Handling a plane is one of the most difficult of all operations to describe in a few words, so we have given it a special small section on its own, which you will find on p. 92.

However, if you have bought good quality, planed timber for the table top there should be little difficulty in getting the edges to butt reasonably well. In such a small piece too, minor irregularities will be supported by the dowels and are therefore not so important.

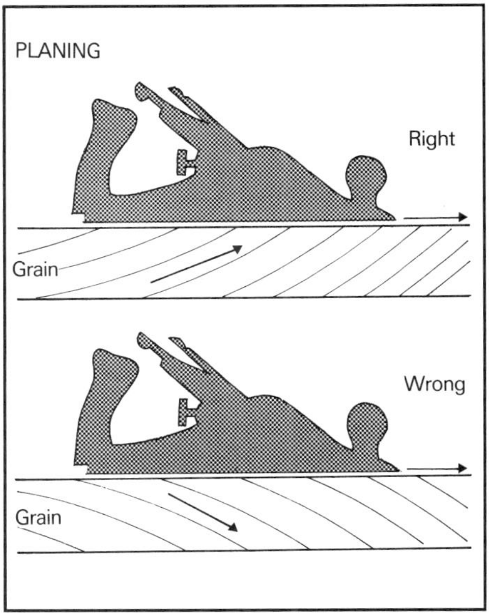

15 Clamp the two parts together again and draw lines square across them *both* roughly 6 in. apart. These mark the dowel positions.

16 Drill down dead centre in each plank exactly on these lines. The tricky part here is to hold the drill absolutely vertical to the plank edge. Take it slowly and easily. There are special guides called 'dowelling jigs' which you can buy to help with this work, but they are hardly worth buying for the normal home woodworker who only uses dowels occasionally.

17 Glue both edges and the dowels as before and mate the two planks together. They need to be kept pressed tightly to each other for a day, which you can do by improvising cord cramps as shown on p. 74.

15

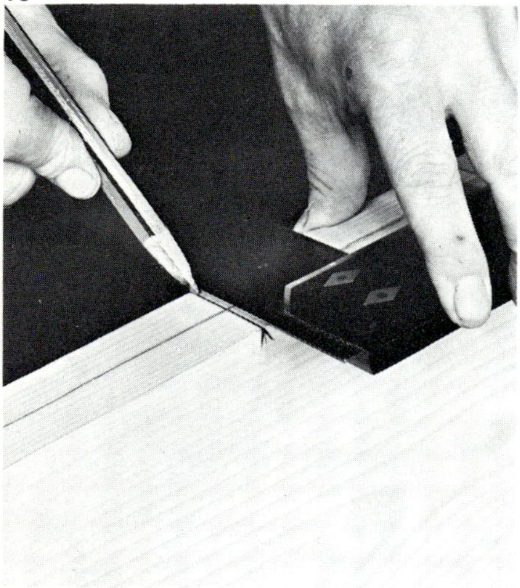

16

17

ASSEMBLY OF THE COFFEE TABLE

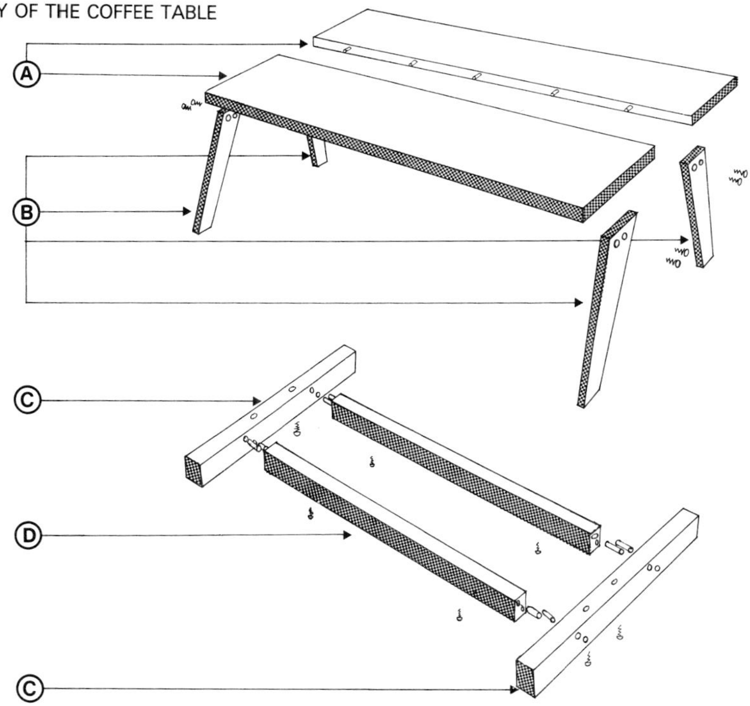

A Table top boards (2) dowelled together

B Four legs to be screwed to cross rails C

C Two rails with screw holes for table top

D Two cross-rails dowelled to ends of rails C

Approx. sized (optional)

A 3ft. 6ins. by 7½ins. by 1in.

B 1ft. 3ins. by 3ins. by 1in.

C 2ft. 3ins. by 1½ins. by 1½ins.

D 1ft. 1in. by 1½ins. by 1½ins.

18 The table's main upper frame is made of four pieces of Parana pine $1\frac{1}{2}$ in. square. The exact lengths can be adjusted to suit the table size you need. The longer rails are dowel-jointed to the cross rails at the end. Tap them firmly but do not use a metal hammer on the wood or you will mark it. Either interpose a piece of waste wood, or use a wooden mallet if you have one. (Really soft wood may even be marked by mallet blows.)

19 The screws for holding on the table top will pass upwards through this frame, so drill holes for these and countersink them *deeply*. You can use a twist drill instead of a countersink for this, but wrap a morsel of adhesive tape as a depth gauge $\frac{1}{2}$ in. from the drill tip. Otherwise you might bore clean through!

20 The legs are sawn from a plank of pine 1 in. thick. Then all four can be placed in the vice and planed to shape together. Note that a small variation in shape is not likely to be noticed after the table is finished.

18

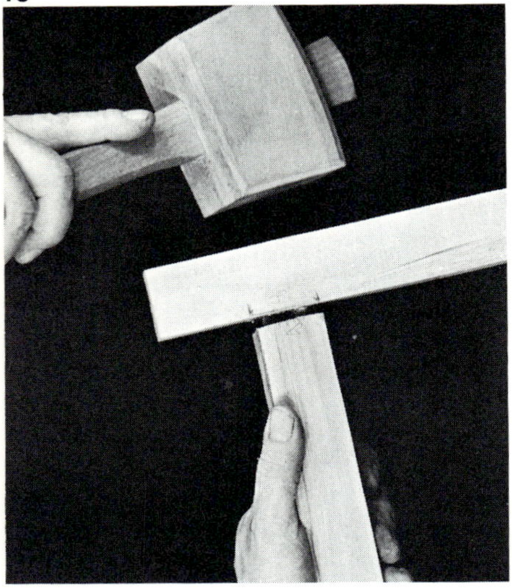

20

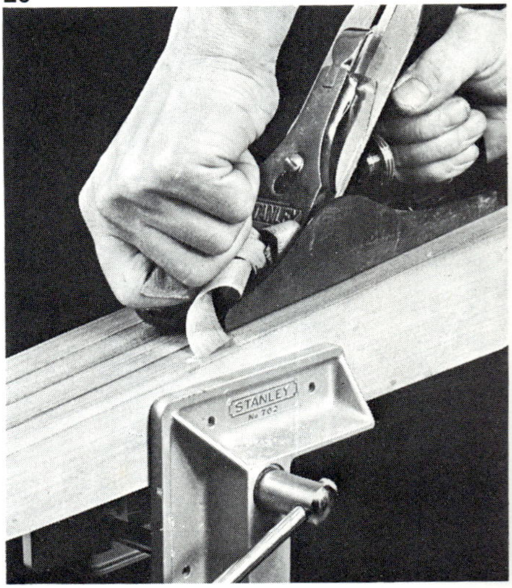

19

21

21 Holes for the fixing screws are bored through the upper end of each. Short, fat screws are best for this. Place each leg on a piece of waste wood when drilling so that the drill point does not damage the bench or table.

22 After countersinking the holes, screw the legs to the already finished main frame.

23 Finally place the whole leg frame upside down on the table top and screw this firmly in place. Watch that the screws do not accidentally break through the upper surface of the top.

24 The complete table is now ready for finishing, either with polish, clear varnish or lacquer.

22

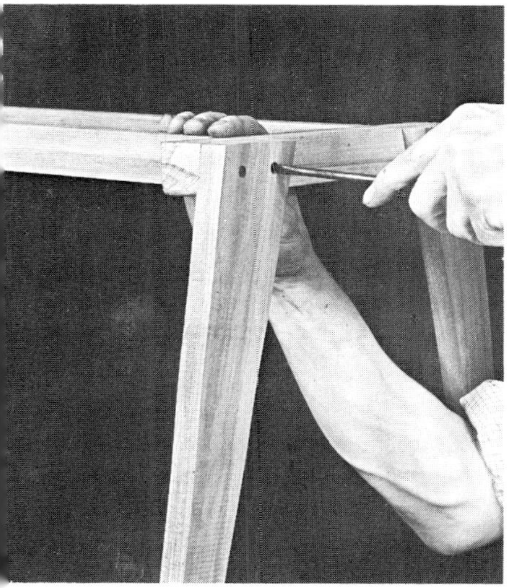

23

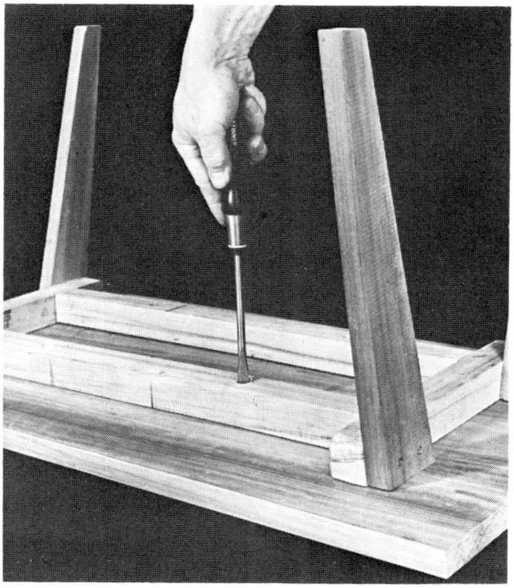

24

9 More framed units and dowel joints

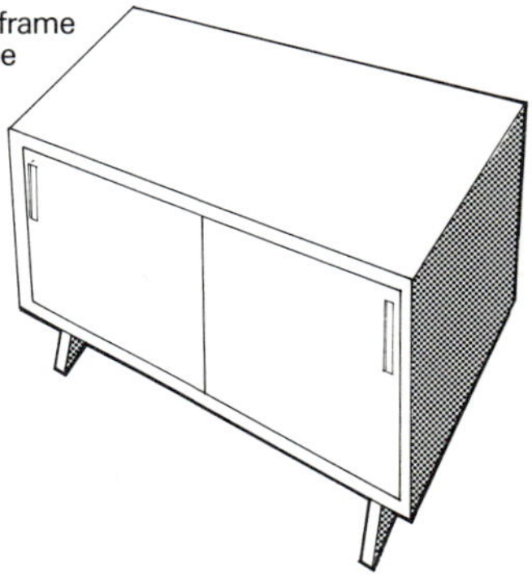

Cabinet raised on frame of coffee table type

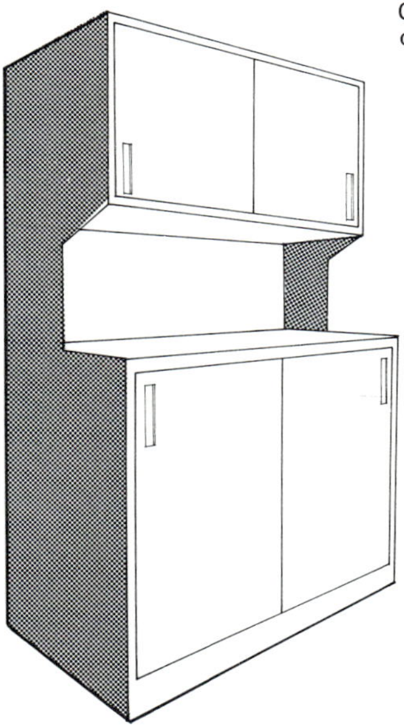

Cabinet made from double wall unit and double cupboard unit joined at sides

Strongly framed unit has sink replacing work-top

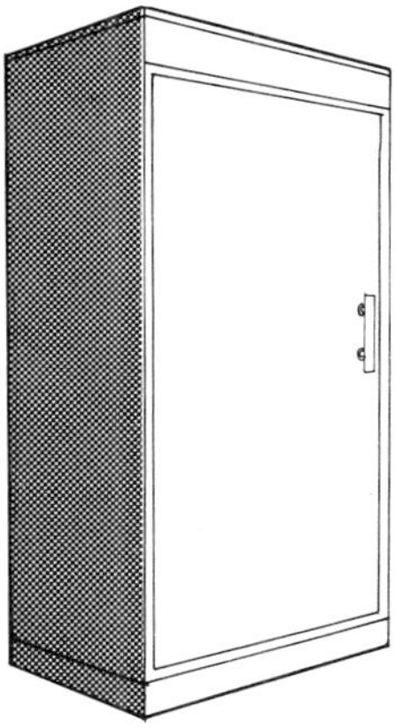

Cabinet made twice as tall makes kitchen cupboard or small wardrobe. Side frames will need extra cross rails half-lapped to verticals.

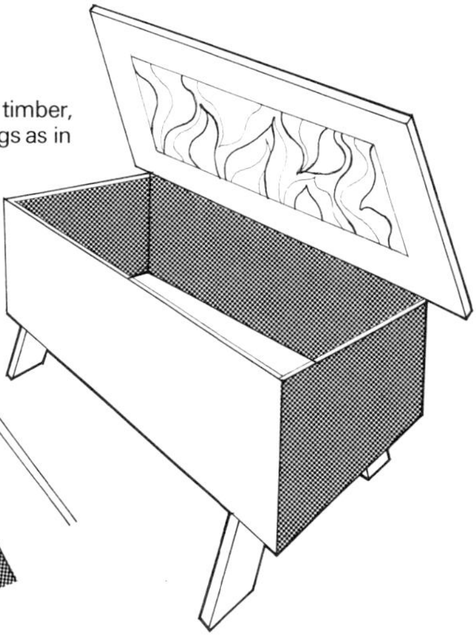

Workbox of butted sides in timber, ply base and lid. Tapered legs as in coffee table

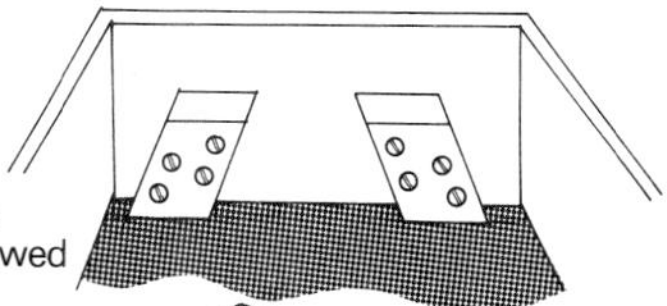

Legs rise through holes cut in floor and are screwed to ends from inside

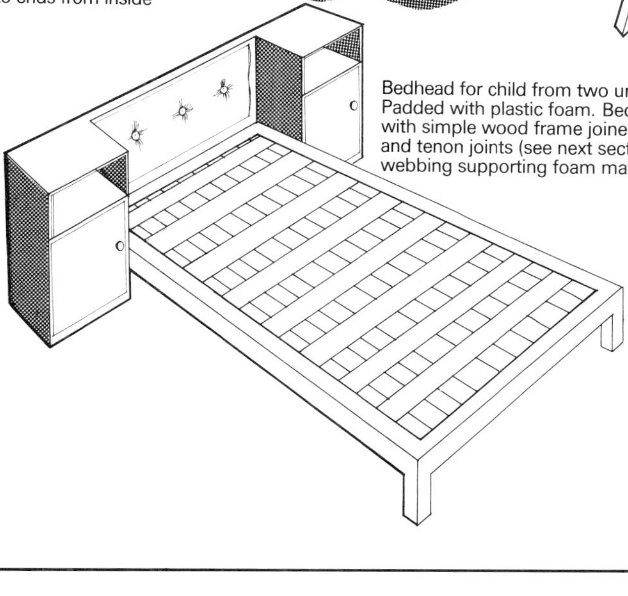

Bedhead for child from two units joined at back. Padded with plastic foam. Bed itself could be made with simple wood frame joined by pegged mortice and tenon joints (see next section), and rubber webbing supporting foam mattress.

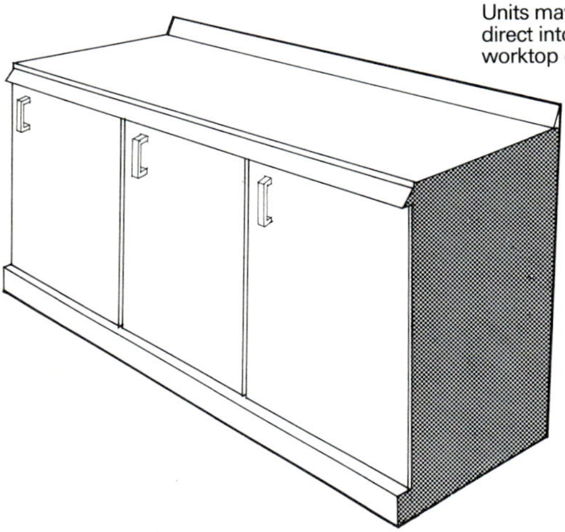

Units may be doubled or tripled in length, or built direct into walls without back or floor. Surface of worktop covered suitable plastic.

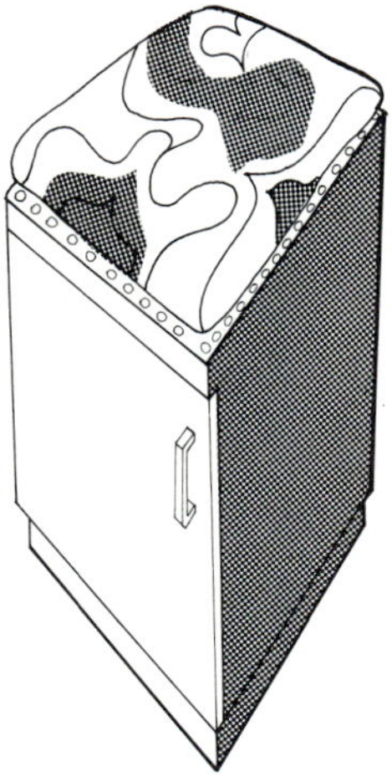

Very small unit entirely in blockboard with padded top makes stool or shoe-cleaner store.

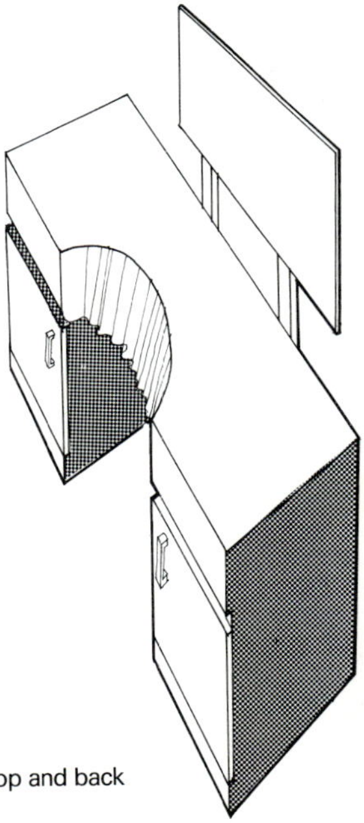

Two cupboard units jointed by wide top and back makes a dressing table

10 Using the mortice and tenon joint to make a dining chair

Although the dowel joint can be used for almost any sort of framing for tables or chairs, for maximum strength and security the usual joint to choose is the mortice and tenon.

This is especially required for chairs, for these are subject to a lot of strain. Also, the consequences of sudden collapse are more serious than with a table!

In skilled woodwork there are a great many variations of the mortice and tenon, depending on the type of wood moulding being joined, the strength required and so on.

For practical home purposes though, the simplest types will serve perfectly.

Strength depends very much on getting accurately marked out and shaped parts. It would be a mistake to try your very first joint on a piece of furniture. Instead, take any two pieces of wood, perhaps 3 in. by 2 in. n section, and join them at right angles, for practice. This can be done easily and will give confidence when a real construction job is started.

Besides the strength given by the joint and its glue, you can often further reinforce mortice joints by wedges or pins. We show how a dowel pin draws a joint tight and gives it extra strength. However, not all mortices will call for this. You may use dowels though, in rather bigger articles like bed frames or full-sized dining tables.

Tools

Strictly speaking you need no new tools for his job, but two smaller items will be found useful.

Razor knife This is a sharp tipped tool with replaceable blades, ideal for very fine marking out. The smaller the item being made, the more essential the accuracy of marking and cutting.

Block plane This is a very small, short faced plane with its blade set very low. It is intended for use in smoothing and shaping the *ends* of pieces of timber, across the rough 'end-grain' and is handy for making accurate square ends in good jointing.

Razor knife

Block plane

Materials
Note. It is possible to make this chair in Parana pine, a softwood easy to work. A better chair would result from using a locally available hardwood with straight grain.
4 in. by $1\frac{1}{2}$ in. planed timber, 2 pieces
4 ft., 2 pieces 1 ft. 6 in., 2 pieces
1 ft. $2\frac{1}{2}$ in. and 2 pieces 1 ft. 3 in. long
$1\frac{1}{2}$ in. by $1\frac{1}{2}$ in. planed timber, 1 piece
1 ft. 3 in. long
36 in. $\frac{5}{16}$ in. dowelling
$\frac{3}{4}$ in. blockboard 1 ft. $2\frac{1}{2}$ in. by 1 ft. $3\frac{1}{2}$ in.
4 corner blocks roughly 5 in. long
2 seat alignment strips roughly 1 in. square by 10 in. long
Foam rubber cushion, tacks and leathercloth covering to taste
8 countersunk steel woodscrews no. 6, 2 in. long
Wood Glue

Cost
Approximate cost 35s. to 45s. according to wood chosen.

We need a comparatively small amount of wood to make the chair, so it pays to choose good, straight grained and machine planed planks. The approximate shapes needed are shown on the pattern (see p. 72) and these are fairly easily sawn out. It is on this type of work that the longer saw becomes really useful, so if you have not bought one yet, now is the time to do so.

All the edges are planed in sets, like the legs of the coffee table (see p. 58). The first step is to cut the mortice and tenon joints to make the two side frames. The back leg, side seat rail and front leg are fitted with these joints.

1 Precisely squared wood ends are essential for good quality mortice and tenon joints. Place the wood in your vice and make a cut with a razor knife at the exact end of the piece.
2 Take a very sharp chisel, or the razor knife, and pare out a thin shaving on the *waste* side of the knife cut.
3 The little shoulder made in this way is

1

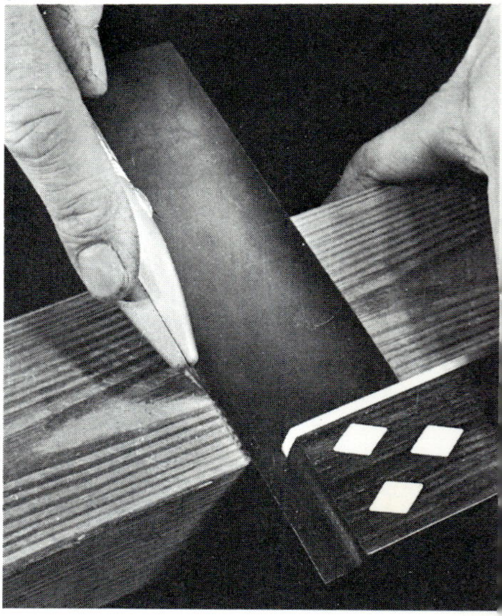

2

used as a starting guide for the saw, enabling a nearly exact square to be sawn.
4 Afterwards the cut face can be cleaned and flattened with the block plane.
5 To make a corner joint, place the perfectly squared end of one piece against the side of the other. All the parts must have well-planed, flat sides. Mark the position of the wood with pencil lines. Check the markings with your square. Alternatively, the marks may be made by careful measurement. However, actual placing of the wood helps to avoid errors in position. Note that the applied wood is not placed right at the end of the other piece, but $\frac{1}{4}$ in. or so inwards. This helps to prevent splitting out when the mortice hole is dug.
6 Take a chisel about one third of the thickness of the wood. Set the two points of your marking gauge exactly to the chisel width.

3

5

4

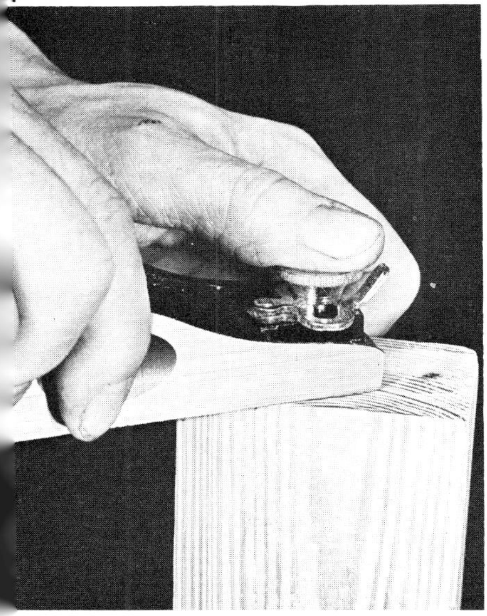

6

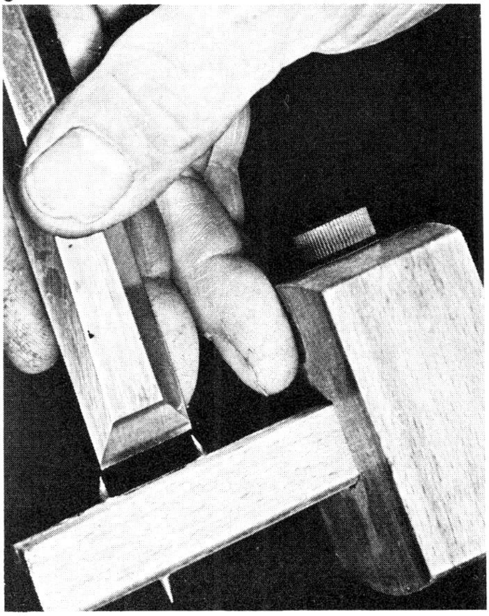

7 Adjust the movable wooden stock on the gauge till the two points make the same holes when applied from either side of the wood. The lines it scratches are therefore precisely in the middle of the wood. As with all gauging, it is best to mark all the wood pieces from one side, called the face side, and to use the gauge *only* from this side when working.

The two scratches mark the edges of the mortice hole to be cut. In this case, the tenon which will fit into the mortice hole is not going to extend all the way up the width of its wood. Mark two lines a little inwards. Some mortice holes are dug out from end to end of the marked out space. In others, as here, they stop a little way short of the cross-markings.

8 To get rid of the waste wood in the hole as quickly as possible, bore holes into the shaded mortice-hole area. The mortice is not to pass right through the wood, so place a ring of adhesive tape round the drill at the required depth. The drill must be *smaller* than the mortice width.

7

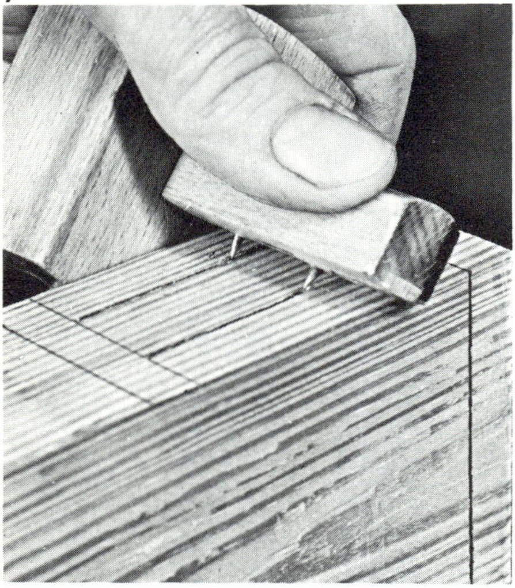

8

9

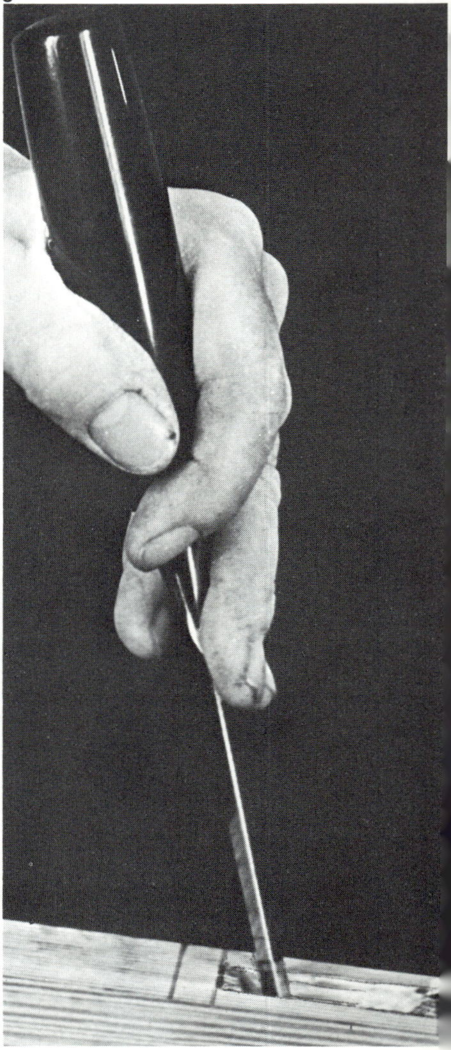

9 Now take your chisel and chop away the inner parts of the hole which the drill has not removed. You can use a hammer if the chisel has solid plastic handles, but use a mallet if the handles are wooden. Start chopping towards the middle of the mortice hole down to the full depth needed.

10 Gradually work towards the two ends until you can pare down vertically, without the mallet, to give a square end to the hole. Note the strip of tape acting as a depth gauge.

11 With the mortice cut, turn to the other piece of wood and make the tenon to fit into it. Gauge the ends with the unaltered marking gauge, from the 'face' side. The gauge may be pushed or pulled to suit the piece being marked.

12 Shade the waste parts with pencil and saw the waste away. Start with an angled cut exactly as we showed earlier for the half-lap joint. (See p. 40.)

10

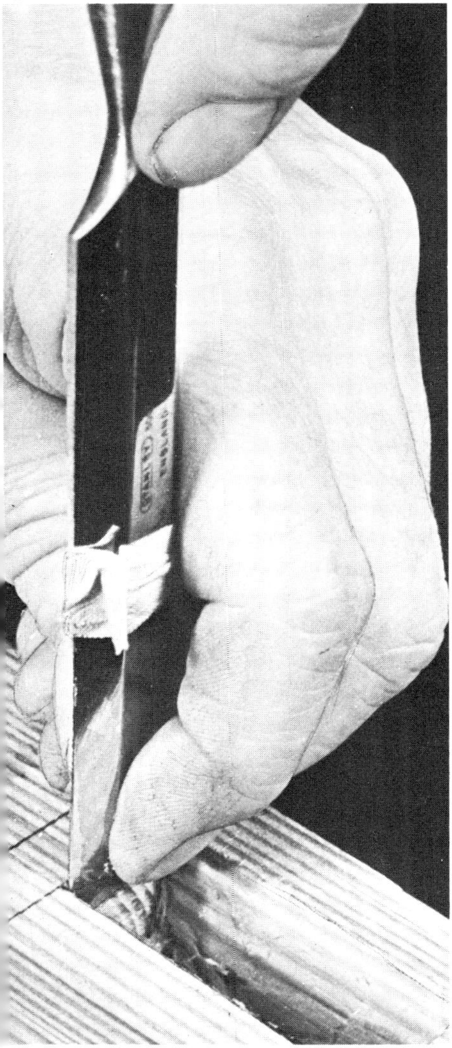

11

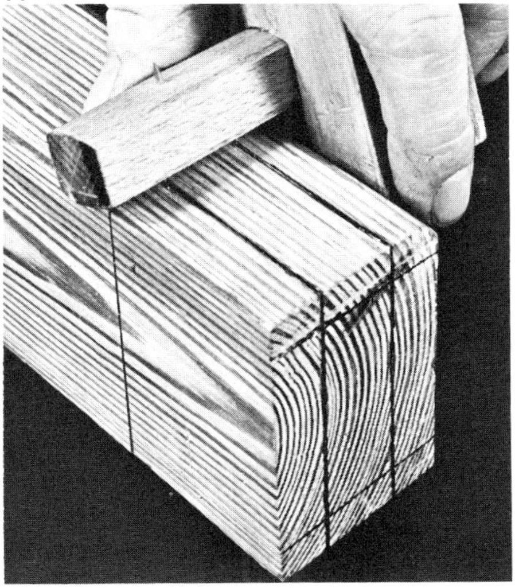

12

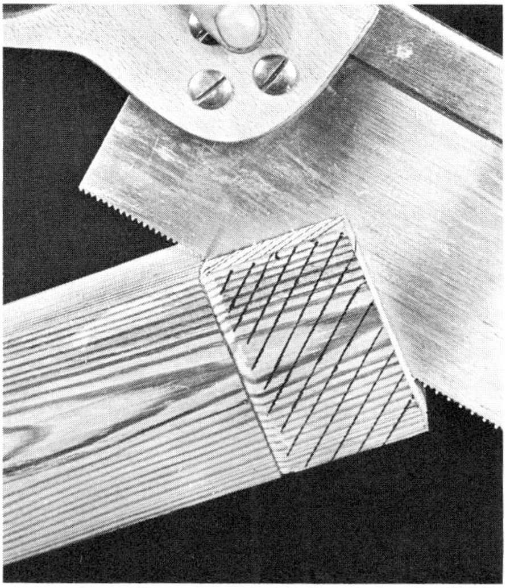

13 Cut through to remove the waste on the flat sides of the wood.
14 Mark the sides of the tenon to show the amount of wood to be cut away to match the mortice hole exactly and saw all this away as above.

15 If all the sawing has been done correctly, on the waste side of the wood in each case, the tenon will still be slightly too large to fit into the mortice hole. Pare the faces perfectly flat and smooth . . .
16 . . . and make certain, too, that the joint face is dead flat and vertical to the sides. Do not use sandpaper for this sort of smoothing or you will probably round off the tenon edges, weakening it considerably.

13

15

14

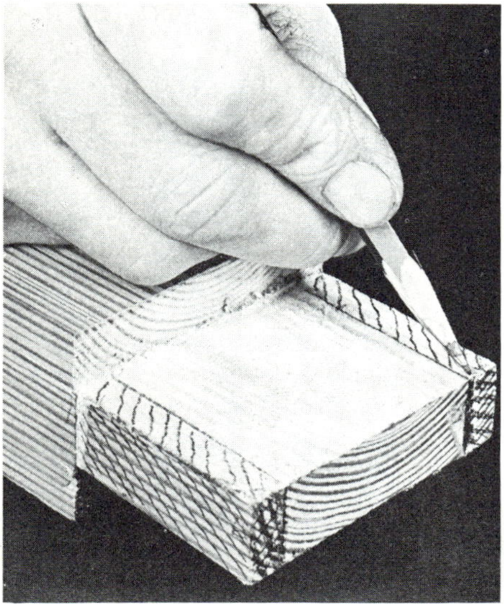

16

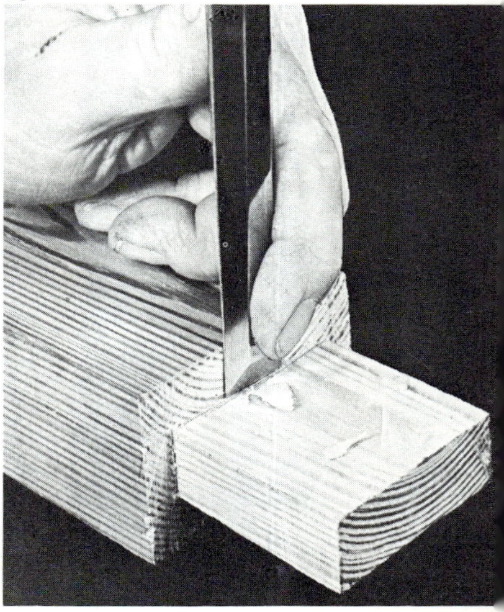

17 As a final refinement you can shave a fraction off the very edge of the tenon tip to ease its entry into the mortice hole.
18 The tenon should be a firm, hand-press fit into the mortice and . . .

19 . . . should become squarely seated with only a light blow from the mallet.
20 Now the joint faces can be glued and the joint finally assembled. At last, the extra length on the mortice end is sawn off . . .

17

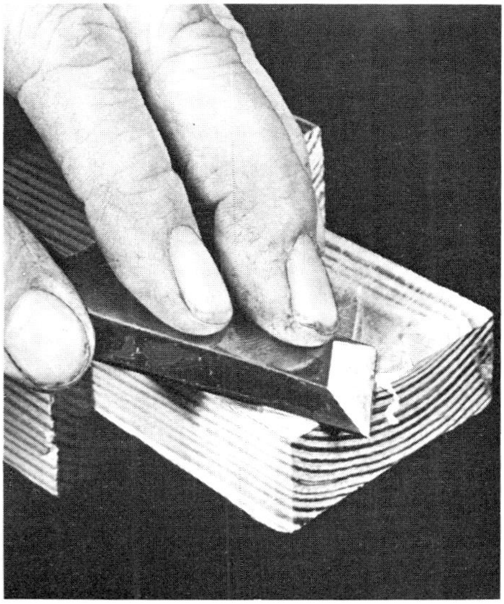

19

18

20

21 . . . and planed dead square and smooth with the block plane.

1 You can add a dowel pin as an extra reinforcement to a large mortice and tenon joint. Before finally assembling the joint, bore a hole as large as your dowel right through the mortice from side to side.

2 Slide the tenon into place and mark its sides through the hole. It is often handiest to use the drill tip but a pencil mark is used here for clarity.

21

1

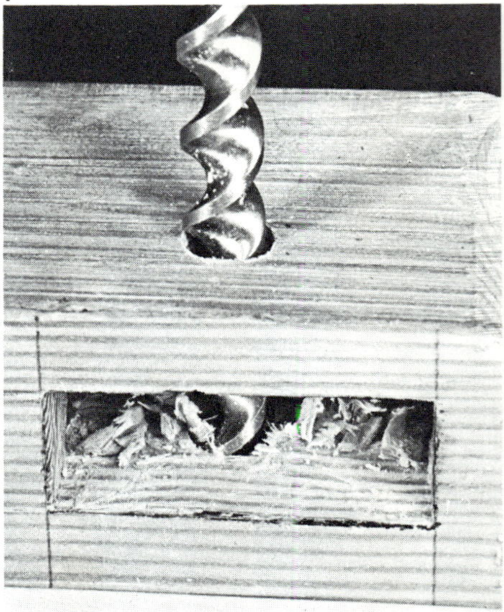

2

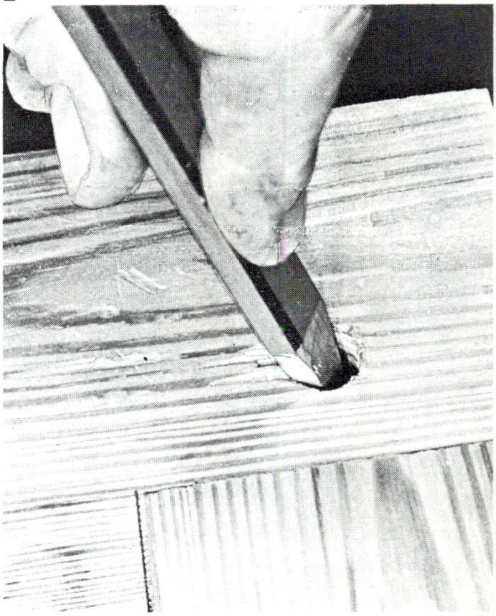

3 Extract the tenon and drill through this too, but *not* dead on the hole marking. Instead, make the hole a small fraction inwards (away from the tenon end).
4 Assemble and glue the joint, and taper the end of your dowel pin.

5 As this is driven through the *slightly offset* centre hole on the tenon it will draw this very tightly indeed into the mortice hole.
6 Cut the dowel off flush at both sides and smooth it down.

3

4

5

6

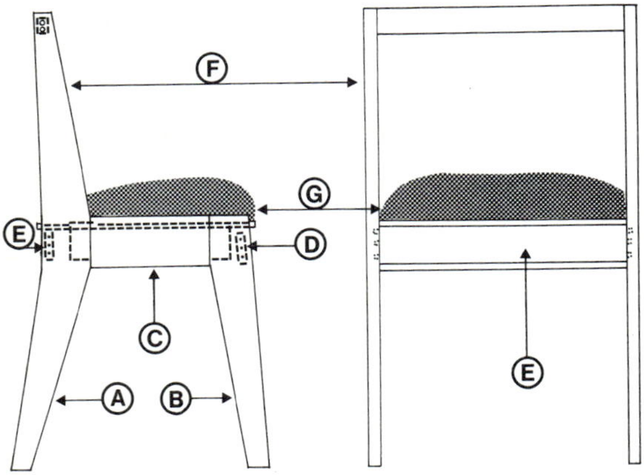

Note. Top of rail D is ¾ in. lower than top of rails C

Note. Top of rail E is 1¼ in. lower than top of rails C

Exploded view of basic chair frame

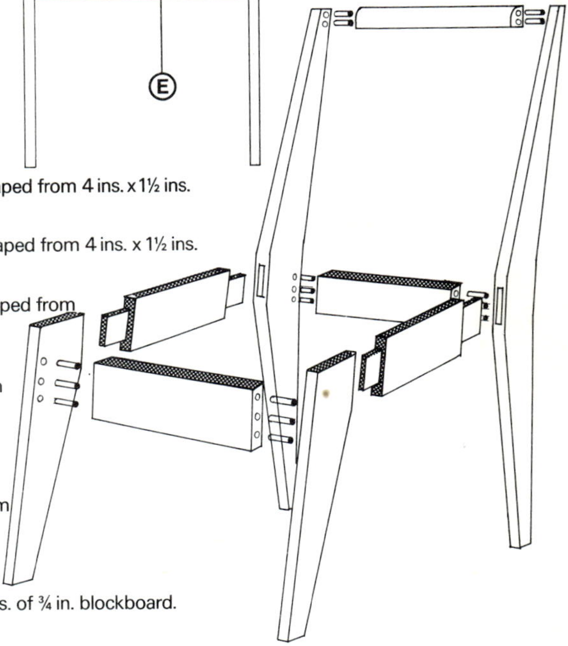

A Rear legs (2) 2 ft. 8 ins. tall, shaped from 4 ins. x 1½ ins. with mortice for rail C

B Front legs (2) 1 ft. 6 ins. tall, shaped from 4 ins. x 1½ ins. with mortice for rail C

C Side rails (2) 14½ ins. long, shaped from 4 ins. x 1½ ins. with tenons to A and B

D Front rail (1) 1 ft. 3 ins. long with three dowels into front legs B

E Rear rail (1) 1 ft. 3 ins. long with three dowels into rear legs A.

F Back rest (1) 1 ft. 3 ins. long from 1½ ins. x 1½ ins. wood with rounded front and dowelled into tops of legs A

G Seat (1) 1 ft. 2½ ins. x 1 ft. 3½ ins. of ¾ in. blockboard. Covered in padded foam.

1 After careful checking for perfect fit, the rear leg and seat side-rail are slid together using slow setting glue.
2 Next fit the front leg and repeat the whole operation to make the other side frame.

3 The side frames are joined by cross-rails at seat level, but slightly lower than the tops of the seat side rails. Three dowels are used for the joint, though you could, with more work, have used tenon joints here.
4 The square section cross rail at the top of the back is fitted at the same time, also with dowels. To give a comfortable leaning place the upper front edge of this is rounded and smoothed. This is done most easily with a Surform tool.

1

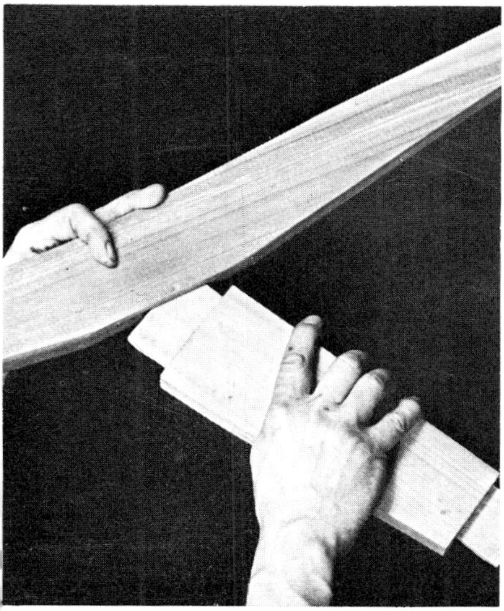

2

3

4

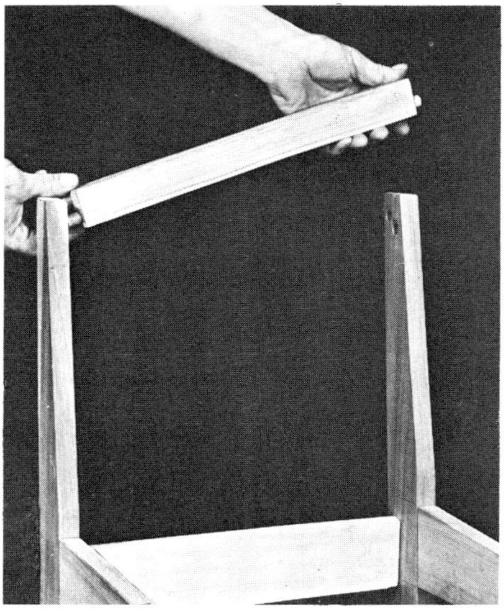

5 The parts must be held tightly together for a day while the glue sets. The simplest way to arrange this is to place waste pieces of wood outside the frame parts and tie them together with strong cords. The cords are tightened by twisting a stick through them. The whole framing can be secured by using several such clamping cords. Check the completed framing for squareness after the final tightening.

6 Once the glue has set the corners of the seat can be reinforced with triangular pieces of wood. These are screwed through into the seat rails. Note that in these pieces the grain *must* run parallel to the longest side.

7 The seat itself is just blockboard cut to fit between the frame sides with $\frac{1}{4}$ in. to spare. Drill several $\frac{1}{2}$ in. holes through this before fitting the foam rubber padding, to allow air to be squeezed out when the seat is sat on.

5

6

7

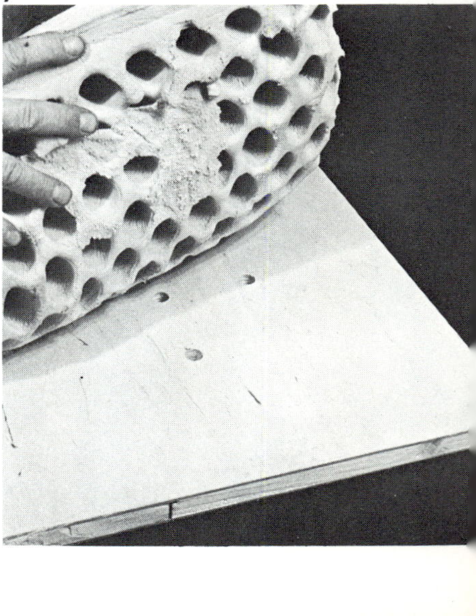

8 With the foam cushion, available in many shapes, sizes and thicknesses, in place, the leathercloth covering is spread over. You need a generous overlap at every side.

9 Turn all edges over and under, and use blue steel tacks to fasten the cloth to the blockboard. The corners are mitre folded as neatly as possible.

10 Sideways movement is prevented by the frame sides. To prevent backwards and forwards shifting, screw short lengths of thin wood to the front and back underside. The seat will then fit into the frame without further fastening and can easily be removed for cleaning.

It is a common fault of dining seats that the padding is too thin. We prefer a more 'dumpy' padding so we used a fairly thick foam cushion. This is, of course, a matter of taste. The wood is then finished in polish, stain or varnish.

8

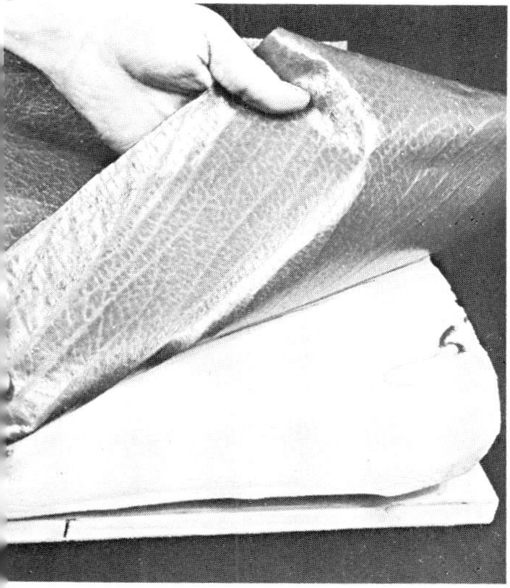

10

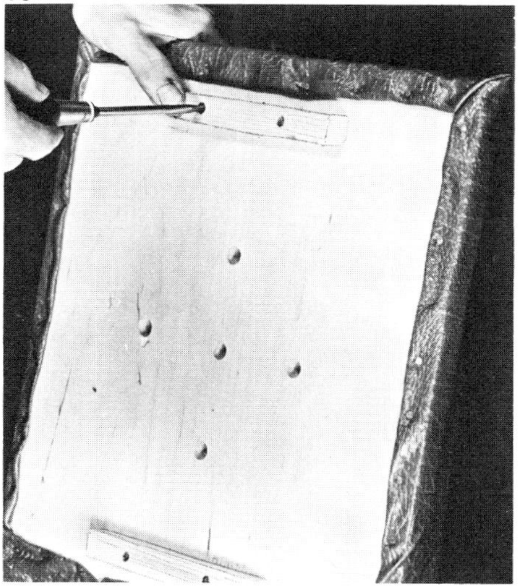

9

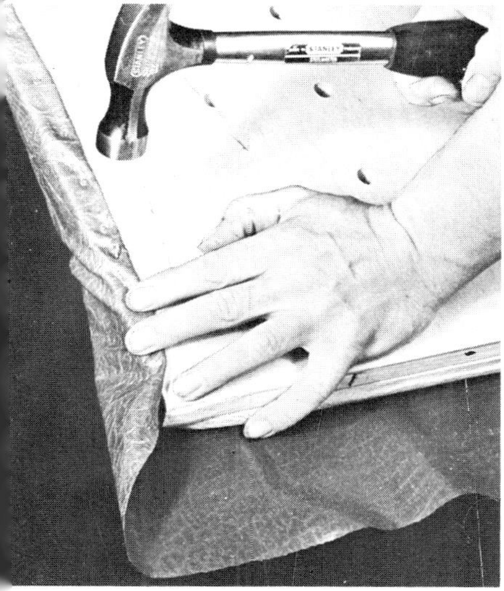

11

11 Using the dovetail joint to make drawers

Most of us will have seen dovetail joints in the corners of drawers. The joint has an undeserved reputation for being difficult to make.

In fact there is no real problem in arranging a normal dovetail joint, though there are special kinds with concealed mitre edges, and so on, which take more skill and care.

Drawers for home use, in fairly thick materials, may in fact be made quite simply with only the simplest joints. By arranging the four sides to make butt joints, and glueing and dovetail nailing them, quite a strong drawer will be made. The bottom can be simply glued and nailed in place.

For more important work, and where the wood is thinner, dovetails are the best method and the only thing that is needed to make a successful joint is *patience*.

The marking out *must* be accurately done.

Drawers should ideally run on the bottom of their side frames, so the floor of the drawer should be inset $\frac{1}{2}$ in. or so.

This is done commercially by cutting a slot right round the inside of the drawer sides to accept the plywood bottom.

In home work it is not easy to cut such grooves without a special 'grooving plane', though with time one can do the job with a $\frac{1}{4}$ in. chisel. The simplest solution is to nail lengths of cheap, quarter-round beading round the drawer sides to support the bottom.

Tools

As for tools, again there is no absolute need for new ones, but these make the work much easier.

Bevel gauge This is a device like a movable trysquare with two arms. These can be set at any desired angle and held there by a locking screw.

Keyhole saw We suggest this, rather than the traditional 'coping saw', because it has a wider range of use in the home. It has a very narrow, replaceable blade that can be used to cut out complex curves in sheets.

Materials

The thicknesses of drawer sides and floors will obviously largely depend on the overall size of the drawer. In general, use fairly substantial timber, especially softwoods. The front and back may be made thicker than the sides, but if so, remember that the depth of the dovetail pins (see following pages) will only be the thickness of the *thinner* sides.

Hardboard may be used for drawer bottoms in light use, but ply is always better. For economy, the beading used for supporting the floor need not be fully machined quarter-round, but may be simple squared strip about $\frac{1}{4}$ in. to $\frac{3}{8}$ in. square in section.

False fronts for drawers can be had to match the furniture, the drawer body being in cheaper wood.

Candle wax rubbed along drawer runners eases them.

The Plain Butt-jointed Drawer

The front is made double by applying a decorative front panel, as shown on p. 46, screwed on from behind.

Keyhole saw

1 Cut the four drawer sides to make a suitably-sized rectangle to fit the available space, but $\frac{1}{4}$ in. lower than the height of the opening. Arrange the pieces so that the sides run the full drawer depth, the ends fitting between them.

2 Nail the sides to the ends with dovetail nails, applying strong glue to all the joints.

1

2

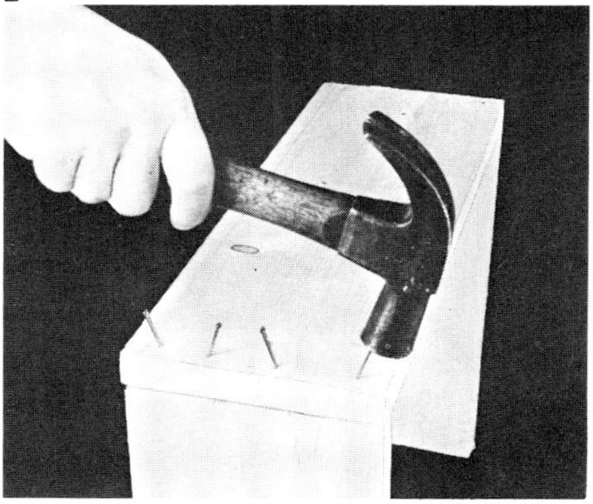

Bevel gauge

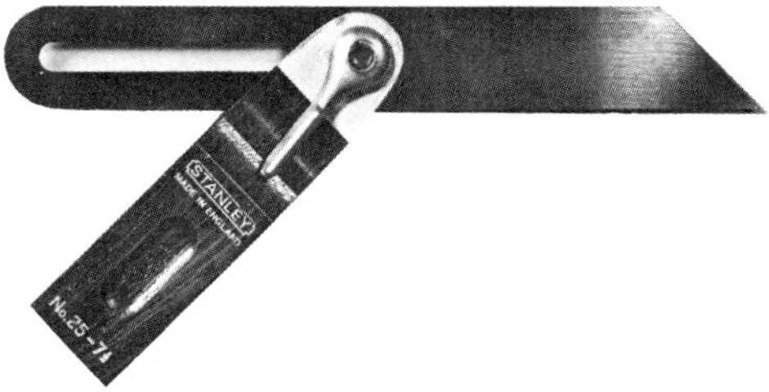

3 The simplest flooring of all is nailed-on hardboard or ply.
4 Use glue and small nails with round heads, rather than the usual panel pins. Smooth the joints and the drawer is ready for fitting.

3

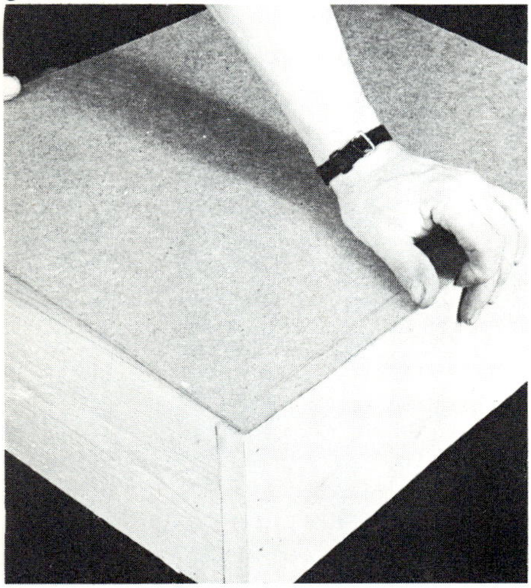

4

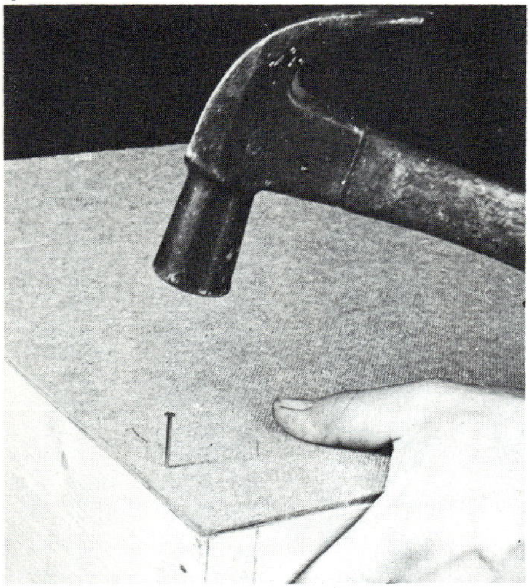

The Dovetail-jointed Drawer

High quality drawers are usually made with dovetail joints at the corners. The sides and ends are made to interlock with each other. This is one of the more advanced of woodworking joints and there are many possible variants of it. The interlocking 'dovetails' and 'pins', as they are called, may be of different proportions, the wood used for the sides and ends may be different in thickness, and there may be special overlapping lips arranged to conceal the joints wholly or in part.

Before tackling any of these more complex types, it is essential to practice on some simple item, such as this drawer. The wood of the sides and ends is the same in thickness, and the dovetail is left exposed on all sides. It is actually easier to make well fitting joints in hardwoods than softwoods, the parts taking a more accurate shape. However, by using cheaper wood for your first attempts you will get valuable practice in marking out and sawing.

The key to successful dovetail jointing lies in careful marking out, and making sure that all saw cuts are made on the *waste* sides of your markings.

Cutting wood sizes for dovetail-jointed drawers is different to cutting wood sizes for butt-jointed drawers.

Cut the two sides, the front and the back to the final measurements. If the finished drawer is to measure 18 in. by 15 in., cut two pieces 18 in. long and another two pieces 15 in. long.

In this example we are assuming that the four pieces have the same thickness.

Make sure that the ends are perfectly squared off.

Label the corners A, B, C, D, for easier sorting out later on.

The back corners of the sides may be rounded off with a Surform tool, to ease the drawer's entry into its space.

Drawers like this have dovetails visible from the front. To conceal these, one can make special lapped dovetails, but these are much more troublesome to cut. The simplest and best solution is to fix a false front, perhaps in better wood, to the completed drawer, as shown on p. 76.

1 Set the single point of your marking gauge to the precise thickness of the side pieces.
2 Now mark both ends of each piece.
3 The ends must now be marked off into dovetails. The finer the wood the smaller the dovetails. In our example the wood is $\frac{3}{4}$ in. thick. There are many different and acceptable ways of marking out dovetails, but this pattern is probably the best to start with.

Divide the board-end into equal spaces, the number of spaces depending on the width of the board. We have used $\frac{1}{2}$ in. spaces.

Shade in the first space. Miss two spaces and shade in the next. Miss another two and shade in the next, and so on. The pattern then looks like this.

1

2

3

4 Take your bevel gauge and set it to an angle of about 1 in 6. Then use it to continue the spacing lines on the end of the board back to the gauged line. Notice the shape of the first shaded space . . .
5 . . . and continue the *shading* of the spaces down to the gauge line. The white dovetails become visible.

6 Practice this setting out on waste wood to get the hang of the job. Fortunately, occasional inaccuracies are not very important.
7 Take the two sides of the drawer. Mark the dovetails at *both ends* of them. To save time place the two sides together in the vice. Then saw down the sides of the dovetails in the *shaded waste parts*. Cut down nearly to the gauged line. Do the same at the other ends.

4

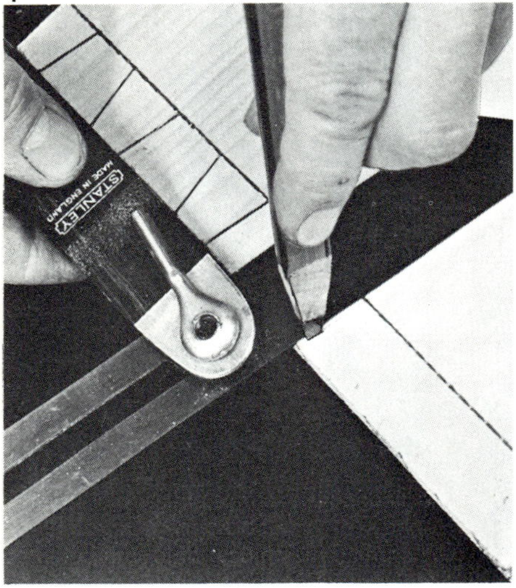

5

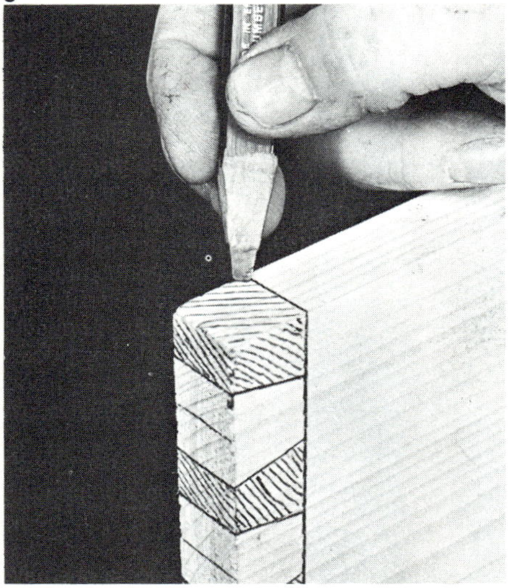

6

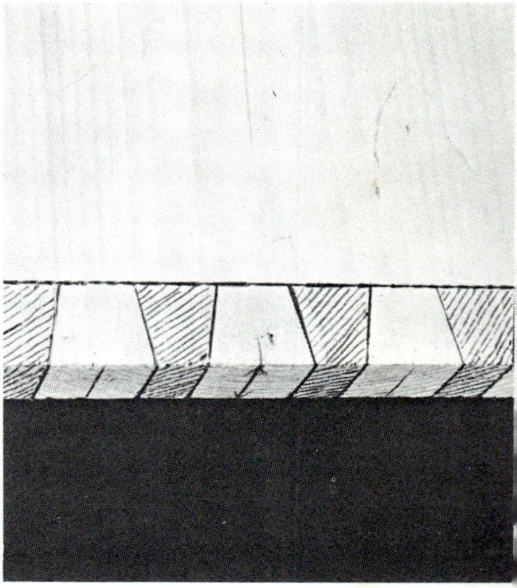

7

8 Use one of the sides to help mark the dovetails for the front and back pieces.

Stand the front piece upright (perhaps supported in the vice). Lay the partially sawn dovetails of one of the sides in place over its end, exactly as it will fit in the finished drawer. Set the tip of the saw in each saw cut, let it rest on the front piece and draw it lightly out. This will mark the end of the piece in the vice with lines corresponding to the dovetail sides. Mark *all* the dovetails before removing the board. Then do the same with the other end of the front piece.

8

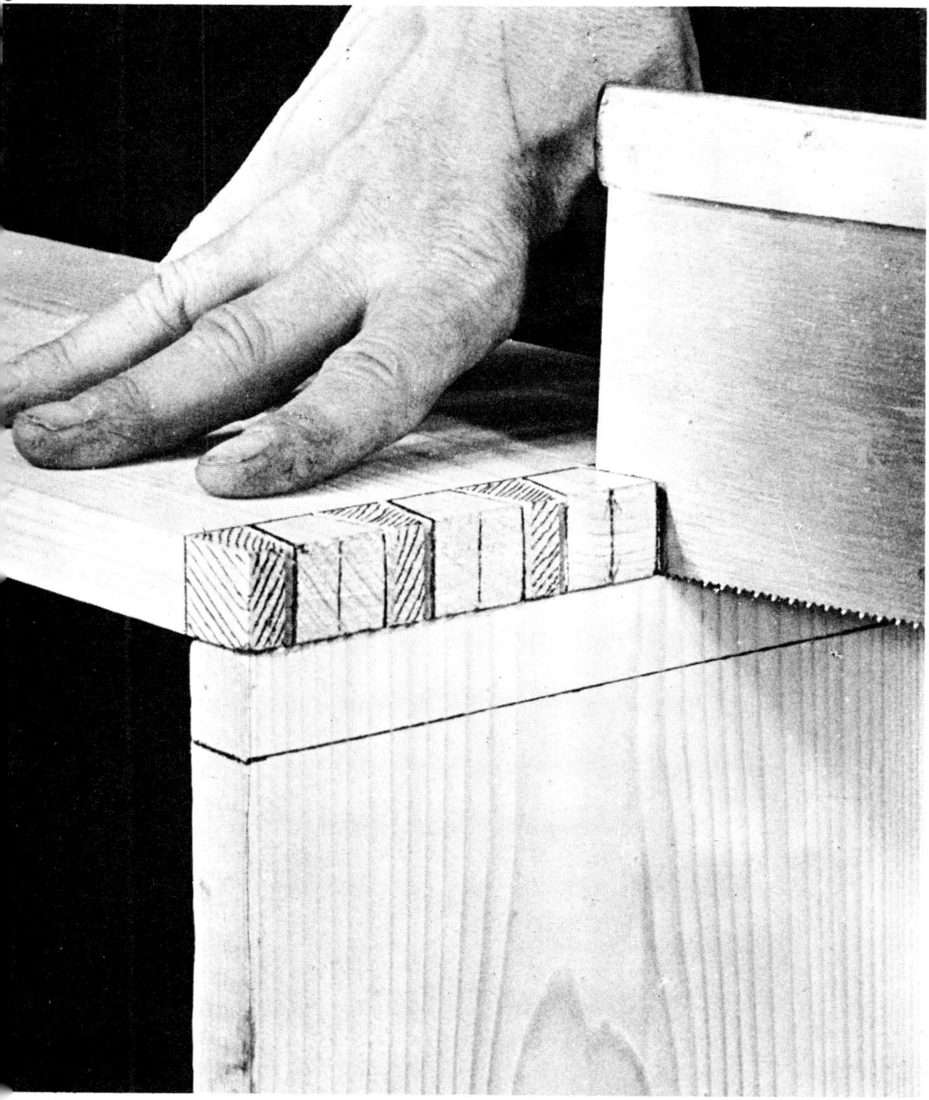

9 Emphasise the scratch marks with a pencil if you want to, and as before, continue the shading back to the gauge lines.

Repeat all these operations with the back piece.

10 The waste parts on the front and back pieces are shown here ready for removal.

9

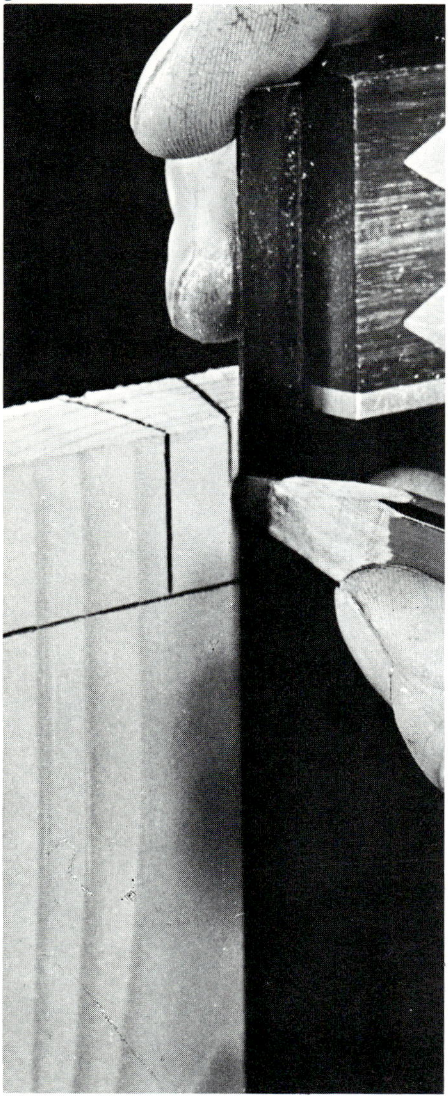

10

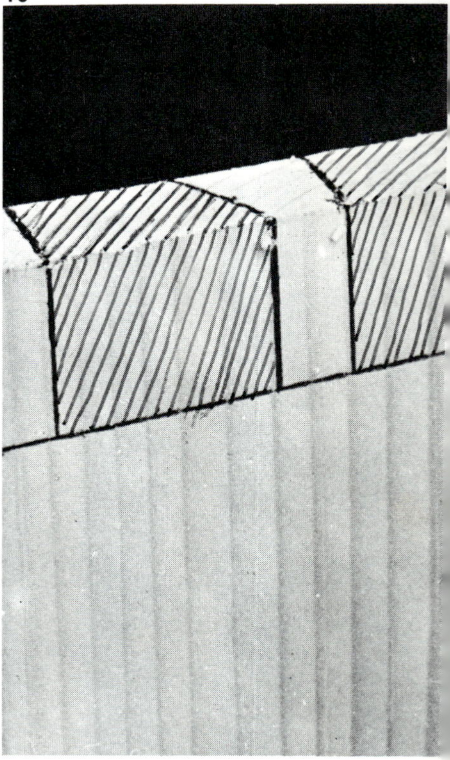

11 Returning to the sides, remove the waste parts. These again are the *shaded* parts. Your keyhole saw will come in handy for sawing out the bulk of the wood.

The completed 'pins' as they are called must show their marking-out lines *after* the waste has been cut away.

12 Use the bevel edged chisel to shave the rest of the waste to a neat, square shoulder.

11

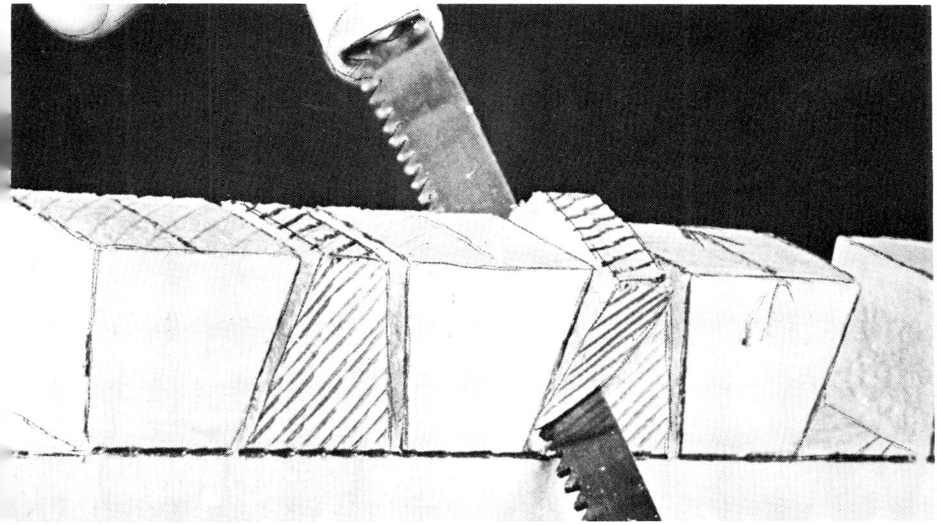

12

13 All the parts will still show their marking out lines after the waste has been removed. They should be a firm fit into each other under hand pressure.

14 After glueing they may require a few taps with a mallet or hammer to settle the parts closely together. Interpose a piece of waste wood or the joint parts may be damaged.

13

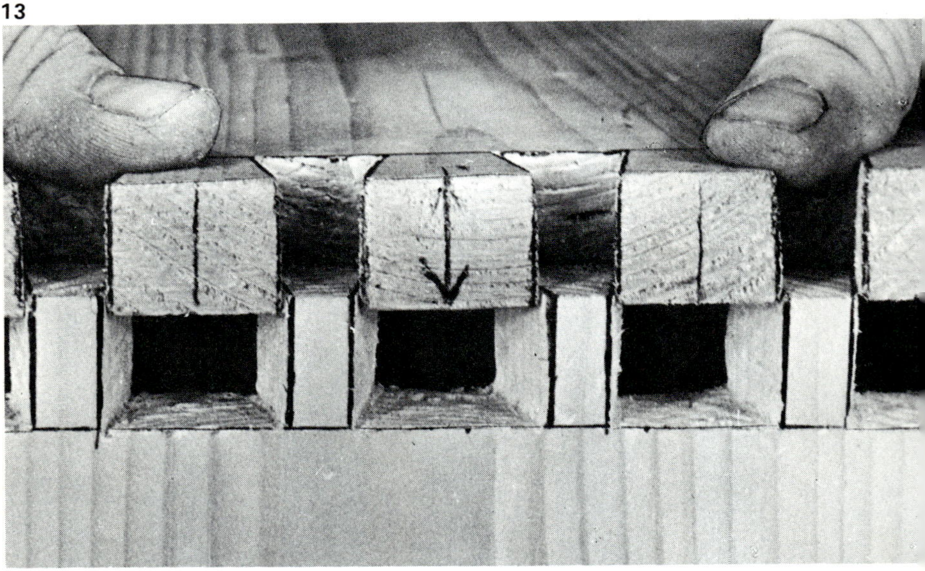

14

15 Check the corners for square and remove any projections with a block plane or Surform tool.

16 It is common to make drawer bottoms a slide-in fit to allow for expansion and contraction of the timber. If this is to be done, make the back of the drawer about $\frac{1}{2}$ in. shallower than the sides, giving this stepped effect at the bottom rear.

15

16

17 Glue and pin strips of narrow moulding to the drawer sides $\frac{1}{4}$ in. below this space, so that the drawer bottom can pass under the back piece and above the mouldings.

17

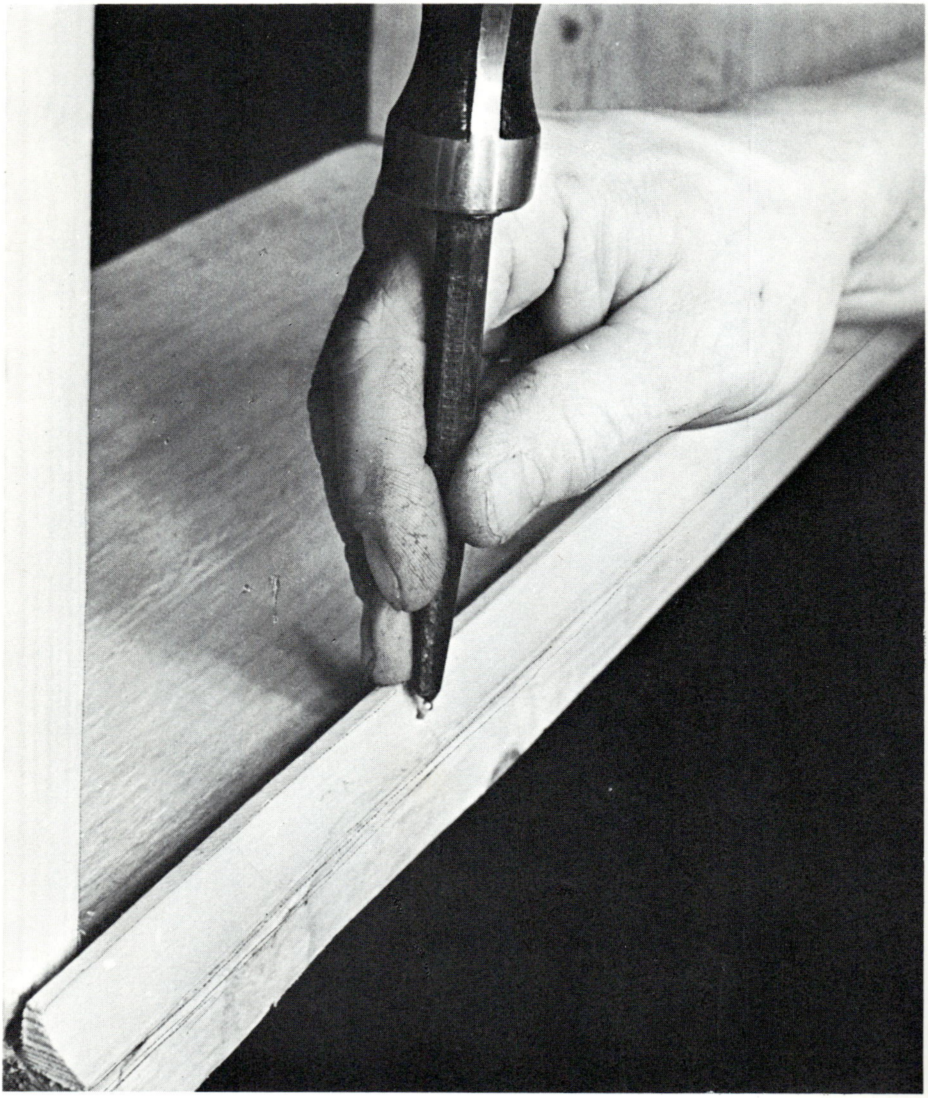

18 The front piece has a double strip of moulding with a gap between to accept the floor . . .

19 . . . whilst at the rear, the floor is screwed up to the back piece. As an alternative to these supporting mouldings, you can chisel a shallow slot all round the front and sides of the drawer, but this takes time and is not easy without special tools.

18

19

Section Three

Sanding and filling

Before you can paint or polish the things you have made, the final treatment of the wood and joints must be completed.

Sanding

This is the basic and essential job. Sandpaper is sold in varying degrees of coarseness. The sheets are numbered; the higher the number, the coarser the paper.

Curved surfaces are smoothed by rubbing with sandpaper held in the fingers, but flat surfaces will become slightly rounded if done like this. Wrap the piece of paper round a short block of flat-sided wood and rub the article with this. In doing so there is a risk of rounding off edges. This is acceptable if it is deliberate and fairly pronounced, but if an edge is *supposed* to be sharp, let it *remain* sharp. The edges of a table top, for example, should be either a perfect, sharp-edged square or a definite round or bevel.

Work along the grain of the wood when sanding. This seems slower than working across the grain, because it is hard to see where you have been. But cross-sanding will show through polish and sometimes through paint.

You can get a silky smooth finish by careful sanding, but it does take time and patience. In advanced work, scrapers may be used for getting a final silky finish (see Q. & A. section).

Filling

Besides the smoothing, there will probably be a few little errors to correct. One of the woodworker's most useful aids is 'plastic wood'. This is a soft material sold ready to apply in tubes or tins. Press it into any odd cracks or poorly fitted joints and it will set hard to make the error invisible. Try to get the stuff down as far as possible, not just over the top of a crack. Then it will not shift later.

Any knots in the wood can be concealed by painting them over with 'knotting', a decorator's material which prevents paint applied later being absorbed by the knot. Before polishing with some materials, such as French polish, you can fill the grain with plaster of Paris. Such work, though, is rather skilled so it is our advice to stick to plastic wood and sandpaper at first.

Finishing in paint, polish or stains

You can finish your furniture with paint, stains, varnishes or polish. Finishing is a very extensive subject and an entire book could easily be written on the subject. The notes below are just intended to help you get started.

Paint

At first it is probably best to make articles which can be painted. Paint applied over softwoods not only gives a gay colour scheme, it also conceals those small errors in fitting which everyone makes in their first pieces.

Remember that in working with raw wood, you will have to give a first coat of primer. This is a kind of sealer for the wood surface and makes a good foundation for the later, decorative layers of paint.

Do *not* omit this primer. It really does make an important difference to the appearance of your work.

The real secret of perfect painting is to sandpaper well between every coat of paint.

When you apply paint to wood, it has the effect of 'raising the grain'. The surface becomes rough to the touch. This is especially so with the primer and undercoats.

Apply your primer first and let it dry thoroughly. Then go over all the surfaces with sandpaper until the work feels smooth again. Add the undercoat, which has no gloss. Let this dry and then sand it down too. Add another undercoat if you can, sanding after it. Then the whole article will be smooth for the final gloss finish. You can even give *two* coats of finish, sanding lightly between them, if you aim at a superb gloss.

As you see, painting is not a job you can do in an hour, or even in a day. Many beginners spoil their work by rushing to get it painted. It will take four days at least to put a good painted finish on raw wood, but the final result is well worth the trouble and will wear for a long time.

For maximum wear and strength, use a polyurethane-based paint.

Polish

Polish is used direct onto the wood to give a beautiful sheen with long lasting qualities. The simplest method is to apply ordinary furniture cream to the wood, continuing this until a film of polish is built up. This looks well but does not withstand much wear.

French polishing produces very good results but is rather a specialised technique which takes practice and care. You can buy French polish sets with full instructions. Practice on a few waste pieces of wood first.

Polishes can be applied to the original wood, or you can first alter the wood colour with colouring stains. If you do this, the effect is very pleasing when carefully applied, but the stain chosen should 'match' the type of polishing you intend. Some polishes affect underlying water-based stains, but work well with spirit-based stains. Buy stain and polish together and check at the time that they are compatible.

Varnishes

When you want your work to have a pleasing 'wooden' appearance but have used cheap wood with unattractive grain it is probably simplest to apply a varnish stain, in several coats. They are produced in many shades, from nearly clear and pale, through mahogany red to darkest, almost black oak. You should always sand down between the coats, as for painting, or the finished result will have a rough, irritating surface feel and will collect dust at an alarming rate.

If the wood you have used *is* pleasing in colour and grain, you can use a perfectly clear varnish.

Some modern varnishes need special preparation, so discuss the requirements for undercoating and priming with your paint supplier.

As a final coating over paint, varnish or many layers of polish, apply perfectly transparent hard-wearing lacquers to give a brilliant gloss. These tend to be expensive but certainly add life to the original finish.

Choosing working surfaces

Working surfaces must be hard wearing, easily cleaned and hygienic. Plastic has now become almost universal, and the only real question is how to apply it.

Plastics are available in self-adhesive sheets, as coatings to plywood or other boards, or as prepared thin sheets for sticking down. There are also plastic paints which are very tough indeed.

Plastic is a general name. Not all plastics are by any means the same, so it is not enough just to apply the first variety that comes to hand on to a surface where hot pans are likely to be placed.

For general use, where wear is not hard, such as an easy-to-clean surface for shelves, self-adhesive sheet has much to commend it. Properly applied to a smooth dry surface it will last for years. The colours and patterns now obtainable are similar to those of the very much more expensive solid sheeting. In planning a kitchen, for instance, it is a sensible measure to choose patterns which are duplicated both in self-adhesive rolls and in the tough sheets. In this way you can match up shelf surfaces, door fronts, hard wearing work-tops for cabinets and so on without being forced to buy the dearest sheets for everywhere.

Solid sheeting like Formica, which is almost indestructible and remains attractive virtually for ever, is applied to any smooth, solid surface, such as blockboard, by Contact Adhesive. You should guide it into place exactly in the way we show for the contact glueing of backs on pp. 32–3.

Ready-surfaced boards are useful for doors, especially the outer faces of framed double-skin doors.

There is one disadvantage with all these very tough surfaces that is not immediately obvious. This is simply their permanence! It is very important to choose the right colours at the start, as you are going to be stuck with them for years. If you apply a bright red Formica to all your kitchen work tops, you are going to find it difficult to make any great change in your kitchen colour scheme. It is best to choose neutral shades, black and white mottle, white, grey texture and so on, for the long-life surfaces. These will blend happily with any colour alterations you may want to make later.

By far the cheapest way to get tough working surfaces is to use paint, using one of the special Polyurethane based plastic paints, carefully sandpapered down between coats. Give sheet blockboard several coats of this and you will have a gay, extremely tough and easy-to-clean surface at a very low price. Moreover, it can be as bright as you like because it can always be repainted later. But you must be prepared to work at the finishing. Repeated sanding between coats, as we describe in our section on finishing, will be called for.

To sum up, paint is versatile, tough and cheap. Self-adhesive rolls of plastic are satisfactory where wear is not great, but if you choose a matching sheet plastic such as Formica to use on those parts that *do* take rough usage, you will have made the best of both worlds.

Nails and screws

Nails
In indoor work small nails are used mainly to attach sheet materials to frames. They can also be used though, in 'dovetail-nailing' to strengthen plain butt joints.

Nails may be round, with round, flat heads, or oval, with oval heads.

Round nails split wood more easily but they do grip sheets well. Ovals should be used in jointing to reduce the risk of splitting. Blunt the tip with a sharp blow of the hammer before driving a nail into thin wood. This makes it cut through the wood fibres rather than force them apart in splits.

Where fastenings are made into the end grain of wood, that is, into the sawn-off ends of timber, nails often hold better than screws, which tend to chew out the wood rather than grip it.

Screws
Screws are made of steel or brass. The heads may differ in shape, the main sorts being round head, which is a dome shape; countersunk head, which is designed to fit into a hollow cut in the wood surface; and raised head, which combines the two, being partly countersunk but with a raised, slightly domed head. These look less clumsy than the full round head type.

Steel is by far the stronger material, but rusts in damp conditions and may stain some hardwoods. Brass is rustproof, more expensive and weaker, and so it pays to drive in a steel screw first, to make a thread, before finally using a brass one.

The commonest error when joining two pieces of wood with a screw is to get the screw tightly jammed in the upper piece. The correct procedure is to make a hole in the upper piece large enough to accept the shank (unthreaded part) of the screw freely. Then bore a thinner hole in the lower piece to accept the centre core of the threaded part. Thus the thread itself bites only into the wood of the lower piece.

Tightness around the screw shank will put great strain on the lower part of the wood where the thread penetrates and may rip it clean out.

Fitting hinges and catches

There are innumerable types of hinges, doorcatches, locks and handles and it is impossible to give more than the barest outline about them.

Fortunately it is usually perfectly easy to see how to fit most of them.

Hinges
The only point that matters with hinges is where the hinge pin runs. The door will turn about this point, no matter what the shape, size or position of the hinge leaves. Also, the hinges must be sunk into the wood of the door or the frame, or half in each, so that there is no gap when the door is closed.

Initially it may be found easier to sink the hinges into the *doors*, especially if they are covered in ply or hardboard. Simply removing a piece of this covering gives a suitable recess, though you may have to adjust the depth for very thin hinges.

For furniture, choose brass rather than steel hinges, with brass screws. Or there are excellent white Nylon hinges which wear indefinitely and are always silent in use.

When mounting a door, screw the hinges fully in place to the door, with the hinge pins exactly in line with each other. Then place the door in its frame and mark the position of the hinges on this. Screw the hinges to the frame with only one screw each, if possible using a rather shorter screw than you intend to use eventually. Try the door and adjust the position of these short screws till it closes neatly. Finally attach the hinges to the frame tightly through the other holes, remove the temporary screws and replace them with the final, longer ones.

Catches
Catches usually come in two parts, the catch or striker itself, and the plate or socket to which it engages. Fit the striker first, nearly always to the door. You may have to make a shallow recess with a chisel to get it flush with the door frame.

Then close the door several times. The tongue of the catch will almost certainly make a clearly visible mark on the frame. This will help you to place the socket or plate accurately on the frame.

Using a plane

You cannot learn how to use a plane by reading a book. Skill will come only with handling the tool. It is therefore vital to get as much practice as you can on waste pieces of wood.

A plane has a broad blade which projects slightly from the long flat 'sole'. The further the projection the deeper the cut and the larger the shaving removed. Also, the more difficult it is to work neatly.

A steel plane is far and away the best buy. The adjustments to the blade for depth and angle are easily made with turnscrews and knobs.

As we show on p. 55, planes are used *with the flow of the grain*. The commonest fault is to get a 'domed' effect. The ends are planed away more than the middle.

Pressure on the plane should alter smoothly from end to end of the wood if this effect is to be avoided. At the start of the stroke your weight should be more on front of the plane; at the middle of the stroke the weight should be equal at the front and rear; at the end of the stroke there should be more weight on the rear. You should feel as though you are trying to plane the wood more in the middle than at the ends.

A properly sharpened plane is easy to use, so if a lot of force seems to be needed the chances are that:

1. The blade is blunt
2. The blade is set too far out, giving too deep a cut
3. You are working the wrong way of the grain

The longer the sole length of the plane the straighter the wood is planed, but big tools are awkward on short timbers. For average use a plane 10–12 in. long is best.

Sharpening tools

Blunt tools are useless. But chisels and planes soon become blunt in use, so you must make arrangements to sharpen them.

To do this, buy a sharpening stone or 'oilstone', preferably one with both a coarse and a smooth side. The coarse side is *not* normally used. It is for grinding an entirely new edge onto very worn tools, or onto tools with chipped cutting edges.

Chisels and planes are *not* ready for use when you buy them. They are given a partial sharpening at the factory but it is always left to the buyer to give the final touches. You *ca* use a plane or chisel in this ex-factory state but the work will be hard and inaccurate.

Tool sharpening is easy in theory. The cutting edge is drawn along the fine stone face a few times at a certain angle. You will be able to feel with the thumb nail that a slight burr has been raised on the *flat* side of the edge. Remove this burr by laying this flat side on the stone and drawing it backwards once or twice. Whilst doing this, it is vital to keep the tool pressed flat to the stone. The burr will come away as an almost invisible sliver of metal, rubbed off on a piece of leather or, if you are skilful, on the ball of the thumb.

You can buy sharpening gauges to help you to get the correct angle or you can make a perfectly satisfactory job just by placing the bevel of the cutting edge flat on the stone ar raising the tool about five degrees. This will b enough to give that final keenness to the edge which makes all the difference.

Saws and drills are difficult to sharpen accurately at home and we recommend that they are done professionally, at least in the early days.

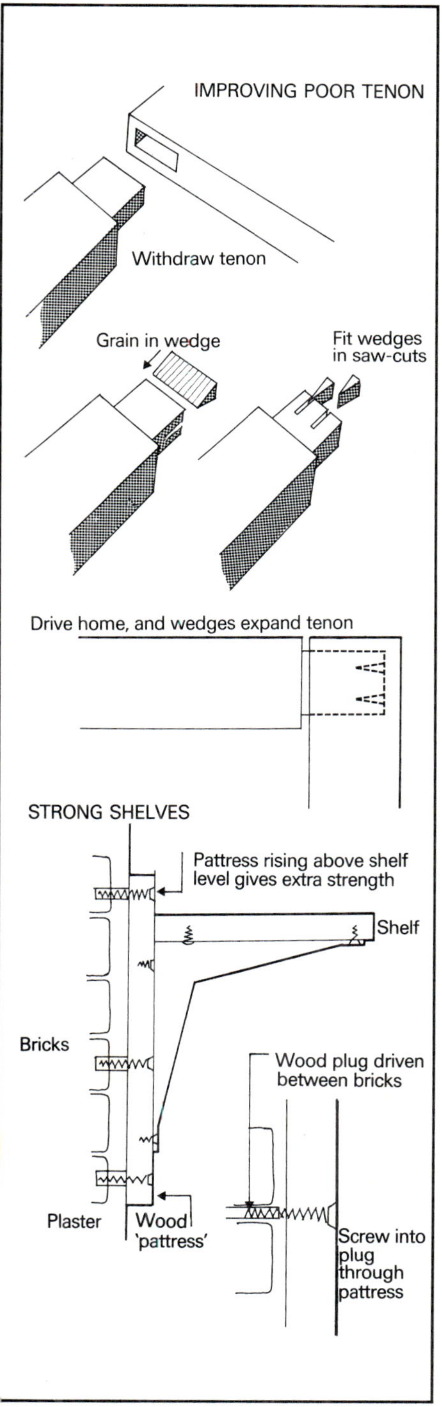

Section Four

Questions and answers

I have made several attempts at erecting shelves and making small cabinets. They *look* all right, but when I measure them to check for square, as shown in your pictures, I find they are inaccurate. What can I do to correct this?
What are you worried about? Home woodwork is not like building a precision clock. If it looks square and level, what more do you want? And don't let the 'craftsman' tell you that perfect squares and dead straight lines are essential. The Greeks built the Parthenon, the finest example of their architecture, deliberately to *look* well, but most 'straight' lines in it are curved!

I want to erect a strong set of shelves in my garage. What sort of wall plugs should I use?
For maximum strength attach steel shelf brackets direct to a piece of wood which is screwed first onto the wall. This piece of wood, called a 'pattress', spreads the strain over a large area. If you have a good drill, you can use the heavier sorts of Rawlplug to attach the pattress. If not, find a joint between the bricks, chisel out the cement 3 in. wide and drive in a specially shaped plug of wood. Saw this flush with the surface and drive a pattress screw into it. If the wall is plaster, make a stronger job by cutting the plaster away under where the pattress is to go, and mounting it directly onto the brickwork.

My mortice and tenon joints sometimes turn out loose because I make the tenon too thin or narrow. Can I correct this without using a whole new piece of wood?
Pull the tenon from the mortice. Make saw cuts in the tenon end and insert small wedges of hard wood. Do *not* drive them right home. Then re-glue and drive in the tenon. The wedges will expand the tenon and make a tighter fit.

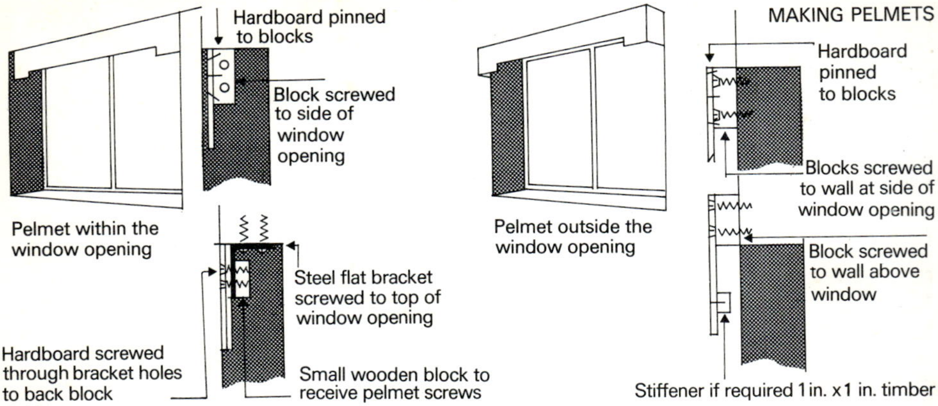

I want to make a large kitchen cabinet. To save cost I propose to use chipboard. Will this make a satisfactory job?
Plain chipboard is difficult to finish off well, being rough-surfaced, especially at the edges. You can get boards with plastic surfaces which are all right for panels that are to have a framing of timber around the edges. Remember that chipboard will not withstand direct blows, or heavy pressure. On the whole, it is better to use blockboard if at all possible.

I have been told that modern glues are often stronger than the wood itself. But my glued joints often fail. What am I doing wrong?
It is true that many adhesives are immensely strong. They only work, though, when the wood faces are closely matched to each other. To beginners in woodworking this is not always easy, and the result may be that the glue is not holding over the whole area. Take pains to get a flush contact and follow the glue maker's instructions to the letter. And where possible reinforce with pins, dowels or screws.

I was once asked if I wanted 'quarter-sawn' timber. What does this mean?
The terms 'quarter sawn', 'plain sawn', 'rift sawn' and so on describe the way in which wood is cut from the trunk of the tree. There is no particular advantage in knowing all these terms, especially since many ordinary woodyard workers rarely use them. Check the grain on your timber as shown in our drawings and never mind the jargon.

I have tried to make a dovetail drawer but the joints always come loose, and I have difficulty getting a firm fit ready for glueing. What am I doing wrong?
Possibly nothing. Dovetails are more difficult to make in softwood than in hardwood, and you may have bought a particularly soft variety. Treat your first job as a 'practice piece' and try again using hardwood. We are sure you'll find this better, and your previous attempt will mean that you are less likely to waste expensive wood by wrong marking and cutting.

When I finally sandpaper my work, I never seem able to get a perfect finish as a craftsman does. Is there some secret to this job?
Always sandpaper *with* the grain, never across it, or the scratches will be very difficult to remove. But really perfect smoothing is often done with scraper tools. They have flat metal blades with burred edges and are drawn across the work whilst held nearly vertical. Like using a plane, work 'with the grain' or the result will be poor.

I find when making joints that my wooden mallet sometimes makes marks on the timber. How can I prevent this?
Interpose a piece of soft waste wood between the mallet head and the work. The beechwood of the mallet head is harder than most softwoods.

I want to put up pelmets at my windows. How do I set about this?
You can make pelmets with any stiff, flat material. Hardboard is cheapest, and very suitable. It can be sawn easily. For curves and complicated shapes you will need a narrow saw, often called a keyhole saw, or a fretsaw. Often though, the simpler shapes look best.

Decide whether the pelmet is to be inside the opening, or outside. Measure the full width of window opening. The height of the pelmet will depend on the amount of concealment you need, usually about 6 in. Make a temporary pattern in cardboard or very stiff paper and pin this in place to get the effect.

Windows up to about 3 ft. wide may have pelmets supported only at the ends on wooden blocks screwed to the wall with Rawlplugs. (See simple shelf section, pp. 16–17.) The blocks will be either on the wall itself or within the window opening.

Wider windows may call for a central support too, often consisting of a steel shelf bracket, screwed to the back of the pelmet as sketched. A stiffening strip of wood along the back of the pelmet may also be helpful.

I have been told that it is wrong to hammer screws in. Is this correct? It seems a much quicker and easier way than pre-drilling holes.

It *is* much quicker and easier, and many woodworkers do so, in the privacy of their workshops! For fairly rough work, especially where it is to be hidden, as in framing to be covered later, you can hammer the screw through the top piece and a little into the bottom piece, and then screw the lot tight. This gives a connection adequate for most practical purposes. Disadvantages are that the screws may break, as they are more brittle than nails, and of course they shatter the wood fibres as they are driven through. The wood may split if it is fairly small in section.

You cannot hammer woodscrews through any hard wood without meeting trouble, but we have put together rough framing, such as used in the kitchen cabinet, quite satisfactorily in soft wood.

Where maximum strength and a good appearance are needed, always pre-drill.

I want to build a small drop-leaf table for my kitchen dinette. How should I tackle this?

Use a heavy ply, about $\frac{3}{4}$ in. thick, for the top. You can stick plastic sheeting over this. Hinge it to the frame of a cabinet, or to a wall, using 'Piano Hinge Strip' which you can buy in Nylon, cut to length. To support the raised top, use more ply hinged down the side as a pull out leg. Note that the hinges of the *top* must always be a little further out than those of the *leg*, by the thickness of the leg material. Otherwise the top will not fold down over the closed leg.

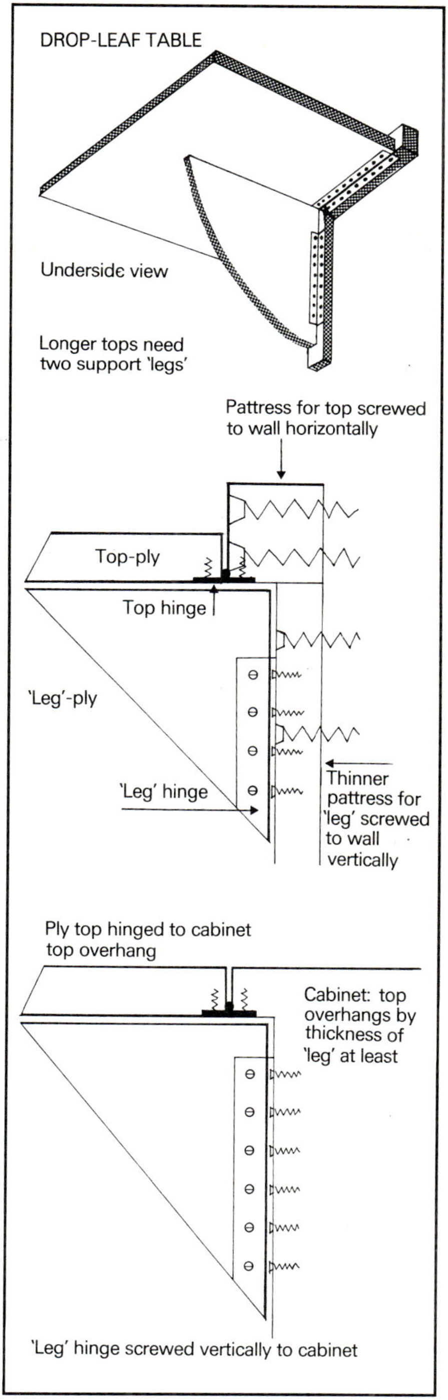

Section Five

A Look at Your Future

Anyone who has worked steadily through the jobs described in this book will have got a pretty good idea of the way tools and wood are handled. As in the early stages of learning any craft, the methods you use at first may be gradually changed to more effective ones, requiring more skill.

Marking out and measuring lengths and angles become a matter of greater precision. A coarse pencil or Biro is no longer even considered. A fine pencil or marking knife is used all the time. The ruler and cheap trysquare give way to a steel tape and a precision square. Where at first you were content to buy wood ready planed, trusting to the accuracy of the machines in the woodyard to give you square sections, you may buy longer planks to do your own work from the rough.

Sawing is also a skill which can be improved. It is possible to make perfect tenon joints without using a chisel on the exterior faces, simply by dead accurate sawing, perhaps using a saw with finer teeth.

A sure mark of progress in woodwork is an increasing concern for sharpness, the grinding and honing before every step, the purchase of special angle-grinding gauges to make certain that the blades on planes or chisels are perfectly ground.

Increasingly too, you turn to the harder woods, finding, perhaps with surprise, that these are in many ways easier to work with and better to fit accurately. Certainly it is much easier to get a tight fit with a dovetail joint if the wood is fine grained and hard, though the practice with setting out in softwoods is worth while at first.

Again, new tools or variants on the old ones will be bought; rip saws, specially designed to cut *along* the grain, for example. Certainly you will buy more holding devices (or make your own), cramps and clips and so on.

Later, you may return to earlier jobs and rework them to a higher standard, using different joints, better systems. But this does not mean that your earlier work was wasted The purpose of this book is not to show yo how to make things *perfectly* first time, but get you handling tools and seeing results. Probably Chippendale's first chair was not s hot! As you buy tools, one by one, they wil become familiar friends, and you will work out ways of using them better, perhaps in ways quite different to those we show here.

The test of our success with this book wi not be whether you can make furniture as well as a trained craftsman, but whether yo enjoy the work, delight in the feel of a goo tool cutting keenly through timber, the first really perfect tenon joint, the dovetail that does not fall apart or collapse at the cutting. This is the true pleasure of woodwork, and we hope that we have helped you to discover it.